ANALYTICAL WRITING AND ESSAYS
for Admission to
Foreign Universities

By

M.J. Ashok

UNICORN BOOKS PVT. LTD.

Distributors

PUSTAK MAHAL®

Publishers
UNICORN BOOKS

F-2/16, Ansari Road, Daryaganj, New Delhi-110002
☎ 23275434, 23262683, 23262783 • *Fax:* 011-23257790
E-mail: unicornbooks@vsnl.com • Website: www.unicornbooks.in

Distributors
Pustak Mahal®, New Delhi
J-3/16, Daryaganj, New Delhi-110002
☎ 23276539, 23272783, 23272784 • Fax: 011-23260518
E-mail: info@pustakmahal.com • Website: www.pustakmahal.com

Sales Centres
- 10-B, Netaji Subhash Marg, Daryaganj, New Delhi-110002
  ☎ 23268292, 23268293, 23279900 • *Fax:* 011-23280567
  E-mail: salespmahal@airtelmail.in, rapidexdelhi@indiatimes.com
- 6686, Khari Baoli, Delhi-110006 ☎ 23944314, 23911979
- **Bengaluru:** ☎ 22234025 • *Telefax:* 22240209
  E-mail: pustak@airtelmail.in • pustak@sancharnet.in
- **Mumbai:** ☎ 22010941 *E-mail:* rapidex@bom5.vsnl.net.in
- **Patna:** ☎ 3294193 • *Telefax:* 0612-2302719
  E-mail: rapidexptn@rediffmail.com
- **Hyderabad:** *Telefax:* 040-24737290
  E-mail: pustakmahalhyd@yahoo.co.in

Disclaimer:
GMAT® is the registered trademark of Graduate Management
Admission Council (GMAC). GRE® and TOEFL® are the registered
trademarks of Educational Testing Service (ETS). GMAC and ETS
have not sponsored or endorsed this book.

ISBN 978-81-7806-091-8

Printed at : Unique Colour Carton, Delhi

Contents

Foreword 8

Chapter I : Analyzing the Issue or Presenting Your Perspective 9-68

PART – A : Introduction 9

PART – B : Model Responses 13

1. Smoking in public places. 13
2. The destruction of natural forests for the sake of land development. 14
3. Following ethics is the surest way to lasting success in business. 16
4. Community patrolling is the best way to prevent crime. 17
5. Do movies influence crime in society? 18
6. Business should set aside part of its profit for community welfare. 19
7. Greed and fear are the two emotions that drive human beings. 20
8. Availability of easy credit make people save less and spend more. 21
9. Advertising agencies follow the dictum, "the heart rules over the head". 22
10. Machines are increasingly replacing men in the work place. 23
11. Companies hiring younger people to save on salaries. 24
12. Societies that do not honor women can make no progress. 25
13. A degree may help a person get a job, but not promotion. 26
14. Governments should spend money on people's welfare rather than on space exploration. 26
15. The human mind tries to find complex solutions to simple problems. 27
16. With the advent of internet and television books have lost their relevance. 28
17. Governments should hand over censoring of films to independent panel of film producers. 30
18. Countries should discourage production of luxury cars because of high oil prices and demand. 31
19. Success means to be able to live life according to one's own convictions. 32
20. Internet is a very useful tool for communication but is susceptible to misuse. 33
21. Parents and teachers should focus only on the positive traits in children. 34
22. Criticism is a virtue because it helps make us aware of our weaknesses. 35
23. No amount of laws can alter the way individuals think and act. 36
24. People hold irrational and superstitious beliefs. 38
25. The wise learn from other's mistakes. 39
26. Availability of easy credit helps us to enjoy the present rather than wait for future. 40

27. Cement manufacturer plans to build factory in your neighborhood. 41
28. Would you prefer to live in a large city or a smaller town? 42
29. Success in life is due to one's hard work and not luck. 43
30. Celebrities complain that they have no privacy because of the media. 44
31. Some people feel it is better to save for the future. 45
32. How would you like to spend your bonus amount? 46
33. Study of historical events is of no use to us. 47
34. No risk, no gain. 48
35. Mid-day meal scheme for school children. 49
36. Should high school students be allowed to wear any dress? 50
37. Should liquor and cigarette ads be banned? 51
38. Has the progress of science and technology made
    the learning of history irrelevant? 52
39. Financial gain only consideration in job selection. 53
40. How should companies reward their employees? 54
41. What should companies consider while recruiting employees? 55
42. Free movement of people across the globe for work or business. 57
43. How should governments allocate their resources for development? 59
44. The most important quality you would like in a good friend. 60
45. As a philanthropist how would you donate your money? 61
46. Is the banning of select programs and channels on television justified? 62
47. All glorify virtues but few live up to them. 63
48. Is modern day life the cause of stress-related illness in individuals? 64
49. Should the death penalty be abolished? 66

Chapter II : "Analysis of an Argument" TASK. 69-130

PART – A : Introduction 69

PART – B : Model Arguments and Responses. 72
1. Tobacco industry counters anti-tobacco measures by the government. 72
2. Can higher duties on oil help in reducing trade deficit? 73
3. Are fruit growers to blame for the rise in prices of fruits? 75
4. The fall in sales of *The Morning Herald*. 76
5. Movies to blame for the rise in crime rate in the country. 78
6. Passenger survey on a leading airport in the country. 79
7. How can post offices cope with competition posed by e-mails? 81
8. Are mobile phones responsible for rise in driving accidents? 82
9. Do higher rates of taxation encourage evasion of taxes? 84
10. The promises of a political party. 85
11. The business strategy of a prominent general store. 86

12. The sales strategy of a leading manufacturer of florescent tube lights. 88
13. Has increase in salaries actually proved counter-productive
for the company? 90
14. Should the age limit for issue of driving licenses
for cars be reduced to 15 years? 91
15. Do high cost homes sell faster than low cost ones? 92
16. Does an increase in the number of travelers indicate expanding tourism? 94
17. Should department stores stock more products for the old than for young? 95
18. Should the State pay heed to the protests over bonus
cuts by a group of its employees? 97
19. Will advertising in *The Daily Mirror* increase business for
the local restaurants? 98
20. Should you be investing in a business dealing with
construction for homes for aged people? 99
21. Will lowering membership fees rather than adding expensive
amenities increase membership for the Apollo Health Club? 101
22. Hiring laid-off employees of a business rival to boost profitability. 103
23. Are customers now preferring the purchase of home
products rather than clothing and garments? 104
24. Can money saved by households through subsidy on
cooking gas ultimately help in oil exploration? 105
25. Should people be buying shares of a company starting
manufacture of rain water harvesting equipment? 106
26. Should governmental spending on food subsidies and
agricultural research be stopped in view of fiscal deficit? 108
27. Does the construction of multiplexes and shopping malls
adversely affect the civic life of a city? 109
28. Do people going abroad do so mainly to eat exotic international food? 111
29. Should the construction of a flyover over an accident-prone
area be abandoned because this will lead to demolition of
some old buildings perceived to have historical significance? 112
30. Does decentralization of manufacturing operations erode profitability? 113
31. Should an ice cream parlor be opened in Snow town? 114
32. Increasing salaries to prevent poaching by a business rival: will it help? 115
33. Can internet based shopping actually result in saving
of vehicle fuel and prevent congestion in New City? 117
34. Will a prolonged use of dairy products actually increase
the chances of osteoporosis in people? 118
35. Does the consumption of fish help cure colds and viral infections? 119
36. Are opinion polls a true indicator of electoral trends and people's desires? 120
37. Are elevators to blame for heart problems in residents? 122

38. Does the compulsory wearing of helmets actually result in more accidents involving motorcyclists? 123

39. Should the construction of a lucrative subway plaza be given precedence over the construction of a multi-storied parking garage, in spite of serious parking problems and congestion in the area? 124

40. Can the adoption of dogs as pets help reduce heart ailments and prevent heart attacks in people? 125

41. Is the level of service and treatment in non-profit hospitals better than in profit-making hospitals? 126

42. How will environment related issues affect the electoral prospects of rival candidates? 128

43. Should the prices of milk be regulated by the government? 129

Chapter III : Model University Essays 131-169

PART – A : Introduction 131

PART – B : Model Essays 133

1. What does it mean to you to live in a global community? 133

2. Do you think that the increasing commercialization of education will rob it of its social vales? If so, what should be done to prevent that? 134

3. How does competition impact the customer and the company? 135

4. It is said that the government's business is not to be in business. What do you think this statement means and discuss the extent to which you agree or disagree with it, with the help of suitable reasons and/or examples. 137

5. Do you think that the primary responsibility of protecting the environment rests on the shoulders of the government and not individuals? 139

6. "Legislation alone will never eliminate child labor as long as there is abject poverty in society." Do you agree or disagree with this view? 140

7. "Education alone can lead to greater emancipation among the poor masses." Discuss to what extent you agree or disagree with this. 142

8. Do you believe that plastic money is fast replacing other forms of money like currency notes, coins, bank checks, demand drafts, travelers' checks, etc? If so, will this will help to avert financial losses due to theft or fraud? 143

9. Do you think that educational institutions should focus only on academic teaching, and not religious or social preaching? Discuss, providing reasons and/or examples from your own experience, observations or readings. 145

10. "Free will is only a myth. Every individual is conditioned to act according to the circumstances created by his birth, schooling, and society in general." Discuss the extent to which you agree or disagree with this statement. 146

11. Some of the largest cities in the world suffer from acute over-population and congestion. Do you think that suitable laws should be enacted to prevent further migration of people from other smaller cities, towns, and the countryside, so as to prevent the problem from further worsening in these large metropolises? 147

12. Do you feel that it is rather strange that great men, who are honored long after their death, were never recognized during their lifetime? 149

13. "Politicians are just opportunists and politics is nothing but the art of deception." Do you share this cynicism? 150

14. "Patents tend to make medicines more expensive and thus out of the reach of the poor. Hence, they should be abolished, so as to make cheaper and newer medicines available to all." Discuss the extent to which you agree or disagree, giving reasons and/or appropriate examples. 151

15. "Weapons are used only to fight wars, yet ironically some countries believe that they help to ensure peace." Discuss. 153

16. "The curtailment of individual freedoms for the larger good of the country is not a sign of dictatorship." Do you agree or disagree with this view? Discuss, giving reasons and/or examples. 154

17. Do you believe that governments tend to spend most of their resources in developing only the big cities, while ignoring the villages and smaller towns, leading to lopsided growth of a country? 156

18. Do you think that the growth of science and technology has made the world a better and safer place today, than what it ever was before? 158

19. What in your opinion is the impact of television and movies on the people? 159

20. Which according to you is the most important skill that a person should possess or develop to succeed in today's world? 161

21. Some students prefer to attend University, while others prefer to learn through the mode of distance education. Which would you prefer and why? 162

22. With animal diseases like mad cow disease and bird flu becoming more and more frequent in the world, and consequently endangering human life, do you think that people should now shift to vegetarianism? 163

23. You have the option of working for a big and reputed company for a lesser salary or for a small and relatively new company for a higher salary, for the same kind of job. Which one would you choose and why? 165

24. Given the choice, would you like to be a self-employed professional, own a business, or work for someone else? 166

25. How does education ensure success in life? Discuss with the help of specific reasons and/or examples. 167

Foreword

It is well known that one of the most important criteria for being successful in securing admissions to reputed Universities abroad, especially in the United States, is the high level of scores obtained in international tests such as GMAT, GRE, SAT, and TOEFL. These tests include the all-important components of analytical writing tasks on given topics. These apart, prospective students are also required to pen excellent essays on specific topics chosen by the universities concerned, including those of a subjective nature.

It is through a critical review of these essays and also the scores obtained in the international tests referred to above, that the university is able to gain a preliminary insight into the mental make-up and intellectual caliber of the applicants. Therefore, the vital importance of critical thinking and good essay-writing skills and strategies cannot be over-emphasized. It is only through this medium that the prospective student is able to effectively communicate his views and articulate his thoughts, in a precise and cogent manner, before the selection committee of the university or college.

It is also true that these skills and abilities cannot be acquired overnight, but are developed and honed gradually throughout the period of one's education. Students cannot master the art of good essay writing, as they normally would, a mathematical formula. In fact there is no set formula for penning good and acceptable essays. Much would depend on the general level of knowledge of the student and his mastery over the language.

However, an attempt can certainly be made to familiarize the student with the art and skills involved in writing a good essay by exposing him to several model essays on diverse topics, which are broadly relevant to his goal of securing admission into foreign Universities of repute. By a careful and diligent reading of these sample essays, he would understand the art of gathering facts and ideas and organizing them in a logical and sequential order. He will also begin to familiarize himself with proper presentation skills by studying the general structure of the essay and the phraseology used. It needs to be emphasized that even the best product has to be attractively packaged before it can be put up for proper display. This is equally true of a good essay. Facts and ideas that are relevant to the subject matter of the essay have to be properly bundled and homogeneously packed in one's own personal style to finally produce an eminently readable essay.

It has been said that while most things can be taught, some have in fact to be caught. This then is the quintessence of good essay writing. It is in this context that I have felt it appropriate to base the book upon the actual requirements of the relevant tests like GMAT, GRE, SAT, and TOEFL, together with model essays from a wide spectrum of top Universities, especially those from the US. In this way, I hope that the book will eminently serve the needs of those for whom it is particularly intended, namely, the vast segment of the student population that aspires to seek admission into the prized portals of foreign universities, year after year.

> The book, undoubtedly, will also be of immense benefit to all others appearing for various competitive exams leading to admission into colleges and institutes of repute within the country, as it will help strengthen their writing strategies and also demonstrate to them the art and skills of effective written communication. It will also be of considerable interest to the regular college and university student who desires to acquire fluency in the English language and enhance his writing skills.

The endeavor will be to present the essays in Standard English, which the average student who seeks admission into reputed foreign universities is expected to be familiar with, while at the same time ensuring that the work conforms to the acceptance levels of these higher institutes of learning.

M.J. ASHOK

Analysing The Issue
Or
Presenting Your Perspective

Introduction

This section constitutes an important element of the GMAT, GRE, and TOEFL Tests. The entire focus here is on testing the critical thinking and analytical writing skills of the candidates. The exercise assesses the ability of the examinee to understand the complexities of an issue and express his views and thoughts on it in a compelling and persuasive manner. The topics are of a general nature and chosen from a diverse pool of issues. The topics relate to a broad spectrum of subjects ranging from humanities, fine arts to social and physical sciences.

However, it has been clarified that no topic requires the candidate to have a specific knowledge of the subject. It is important to remember that what is being assessed is the ability of the student to think critically on the given issue and articulate his response in a well organised and cogent manner, and not his depth of knowledge of the subject matter. Neither is he expected to have mastered any specific writing skills or strategies.

In the GRE Test, this section goes by the name of "Present your perspective on an Issue" task and has to be completed within a 45-minute time span. A choice is given between two topics. Each states an opinion on a subject of general interest and asks the candidate to discuss it from any perspective of his choice, provided appropriate and relevant reasons and/or examples are given to properly explain and support the issue.

In the GMAT test, it is referred to as **"Analysis of an Issue"** and has to be completed within a **30-minute time frame**. There is no choice here. While the topics chosen for the GRE are more of a general and everyday nature, those appearing in the GMAT section are somewhat more diversified and complex and include subjects on general economic and commercial themes.

However, in both the tests, what is sought to be tested is the ability of the student to comprehensively understand the issue, critically analyse it, and write his response in a well organised, logical, sequential and coherent way. It is essentially an exercise in critical thinking and persuasive writing. Each topic presented makes a claim about an issue that test candidates can discuss from different perspectives and with relevance to various situations or circumstances.

The candidate should be able to fully understand the essence of the issue, think about it from different perspectives, carefully considering the complexities of ideas flowing from these perspectives, and then present a compelling case for his own position on the issue. The main purpose of this task is to determine how clearly and precisely the candidate is able to develop a compelling and persuasive argument supporting his stand on an issue, and also how effectively he is able to articulate it and communicate it in writing to his readers, who would consist of university and college faculty, trained as GRE and GMAT readers to apply the scoring criteria, in accordance with the appropriate scoring guide.

Each response is holistically scored on a 6-point scale, as per the criteria published in the official Tests scoring guides. This means that the response is judged as a whole, and no individual aspects of the response such as organisation of ideas, grammar, language usage, structure of sentences or the reasons and examples provided, are segmented to issue points separately. Rather, the scores are assigned taking into count the overall quality of the response, and its diverse characteristics as an integrated whole. Each response is evaluated and scored by two readers. The scores allotted by both the readers have perforce to be identical or adjacent. If they are not, then a third reader adjudicates the combination. It has also been clarified that the responses are randomly distributed to the readers and both the readers are unaware of the scores given by each other. All identifying information about the test takers is concealed from the readers.

More information about the scoring system can be had from the official Program guide. In fact the GRE, GMAT, and TOEFL Programs have published the complete pool of issue topics relevant to each test, and candidates are encouraged to review the same, as they would prove to be immensely helpful to them, giving them an overall idea of the diversity of the topics.

Hints on Writing the Response

These are explained in great depth in the official GRE Program guide and readers are strongly urged to refer to the same for an in-depth understanding of the response strategies. However, a brief outline of the broad approach to be followed in planning and presenting a proper response has been given here to help readers understand how to go about their task.

The issue task allows the candidate to respond to the claim in whichever way he chooses. He is free to entirely agree with the claim, or to totally disagree with it. He can also decide to agree only partially with it. He can question the assumptions on which the claim is based. He can also explicitly state under what specific circumstance the claim is valid. He can take any approach to the claim as long as he does not lose sight of the centrality of the issue. Having identified his stand on the issue, he should gradually develop his perspective logically and convincingly with the help of appropriate reasons and/or examples. He should be able to argue his points forcefully and cogently in the light of his own learning, experiences and general observations.

It is important to understand that there is no "right" answer. The approaches and ideas can be as varied as the number of candidates taking the test. What is of relevance is how well the candidate is able to support and substantiate his own chosen position on the issue, and how convincingly he is able to build up a case for it, and how effectively he is able to communicate it in writing to his audience. In the GRE and GMAT sections emphasis is more on the critical and analytical reasoning that accompanies the stated position, and not so much on the language usage or grammar. A few inadvertent mistakes in the language usage or grammar will not necessarily affect the overall scores in these sections, so long as the mistakes are not repetitive in character or of such nature as to totally alter the meaning of the response or to make it incoherent or unintelligible to the readers.

A good response should be lucid. The ideas should be organised coherently and presented in a logical and sequential fashion, rather than in a rambling and confused manner. The perspective chosen should be well supported by appropriate reasons and specific examples. The end product should be a properly conceived, well structured, and effectively articulated response to the given claim.

Model Issues and Responses

Chapter I contains a bouquet of **49 model issues** and responses spanning a wide range of subjects, which is intended to familiarise the reader with a host of writing strategies. Every effort has been made to ensure that the issues selected span as many diverse subjects and themes as possible from the humanities and arts to the social and physical sciences. However, they are by no means exhaustive, nor can they ever be. They are only meant to be illustrative in nature and acquaint the reader with the broad approach to be adopted in comprehending the diverse issues and writing appropriate responses.

The reader need not even necessarily agree with the perspective embraced by the author or the base stand chosen by him on a given issue. It has already been emphasised that there is no such thing as a "right" answer. In fact the reader would be encouraged to consider the issue independently from his own viewpoint and develop it according to his own rationale and perspective. Neither can the stated facts or core formulation of any response be identical. Every writer is expected to state the facts in the light of his own readings, educational background, and experiences and observations in life. It is this aspect, alone which imbues every response with its own special flavour and helps to differentiate it from the rest.

Hence, no attempt should be made in the direction of memorising the contents of any response, nor will such an approach be of any help. However, it would be useful to critically examine the response in order to understand the accumulation and organisation of the relevant facts and ideas, their logical and cogent structuring, the style of their presentation and the efficacy of the vocabulary and language skills used to effectively articulate and communicate them to the readers.

It is to be appreciated that the candidates appearing for these international tests come from various countries and diverse educational backgrounds. Some of them are from countries where the English language is not commonly spoken. Hence, the level of command over the language will vary from person to person. For those who are not too familiar with the finer nuances of the language, it would suffice if they wrote their responses in simple and grammatically correct language. In fact, this should be the preferred approach for all the candidates, except those who are extremely fluent with the language and would love to display their dexterity with the words, and dazzle with their literary style!

Candidates will also have to properly budget their time in formulating their response to the issue tasks. Within the allotted time span, they will have to read and properly understand the issue and write their considered response. Before they start writing, it might be helpful to make quick notes of the various facts and ideas that come to their mind and the reasons and examples that they might want to use to substantiate their viewpoint. It would then be easier to structure their thoughts and crystallise their ideas into a homogenous whole.

Model Responses

Q1. In many countries smoking is not allowed in public places like roads, railway stations, airports, and other public buildings. Do you think that this is justified? Explain with the help of specific reasons and/or examples.

A1. Ban on smoking in public places is completely justified. It is not only justified, but absolutely imperative. More and more countries are realising the dangers of passive smoking and coming out with deterrent legislations in order to save the non-smokers from the health risks on account of smoking by others.

The dangers of smoking have been fully documented by medical science. It has been stated that more people die from nicotine-induced causes around the world, than from any other natural causes. Those who are habitual smokers are at continuous risk of contracting various forms of cancer, particularly lung and oral cancer. Governments round the world spend astronomical sums on treating pulmonary cancers and educating the citizens on the dangers of smoking. High taxes and duties have been levied on tobacco-based products in an effort to discourage the smoking habit.

To what extent these laudable steps have succeeded in actually dissuading the habitual smokers from their nicotine addiction is a debatable point. But what is of critical relevance is that the smokers have no right whatsoever to endanger the health of the non-smoking community by polluting the air with their cigarette smoke. By smoking in public places, the smokers unwittingly end up forcing the non-smokers to inhale the stale smoke, thus imperiling their health as well. Even diehard smokers may some day redeem themselves from their vile habit, but how do the people who are inadvertently forced into passive smoking save themselves? The more crucial issue is that nobody is safe from passive smoking, be it young children or grown-up adults. The fate of chronic asthmatics who may be forced to inhale the toxic tobacco smoke can be well imagined. If a pregnant woman is continuously exposed to passive smoking, foetal abnormalities can not be ruled out.

illegal action

Many people are greatly revolted by the very smell of the cigarette smoke. Some complain that after being continuously exposed to passive smoking in closed environments, they return home with feelings of nausea. Others aver that their clothes reek of tobacco smell and they themselves feel like stinking ashtrays. → *saying firmly i.e truly unpleasant smell*

Some smokers argue that by banning smoking in public places, the state would be *strongly offending* impinging on their individual rights. However, this line of thinking is futile because, while *not going succeeding* the right to smoking is not absolute, the right to life itself is. While nobody disputes the right of smokers to indulge in their habit within the confines of their own home, they certainly have no right to imperil the health of the general populace by unleashing the vile smoke in public places. Why should the non-smokers pay the price for the addiction of some diehard smokers?

Another disturbing aspect of smoking in public places is that some of the more vulnerable elements among the non-smokers, especially the youth, may be unintentionally induced into the smoking habit by continuously watching other people smoke. This would be more so in the case of school and college students who would think it fashionable and stylish to be seen with the deadly fag.

A positive outcome of a ban on smoking in public places would be that even the regular smokers would be forced to curtail their habit even though to a limited extent. People generally tend to smoke more when they are out of their homes and in the company of friends and others.

Thus, it is imperative that appropriate laws should be enacted to prevent smoking in public places such as roads, streets, shopping malls, multiplexes, public offices, railway stations and airports. This would go a long way not only in preventing the non-smokers from falling victim to the dangers of passive smoking, but also directly benefit the diehard smokers who would then have no choice but to restrict their smoking habit.

Q2. In some countries natural forests are being destroyed to extend towns and cities or to increase the land under cultivation. Do you think this is correct? Explain with the help of specific reasons and/or examples.

A2. Natural forests are a very valuable god-given resource for mankind in general and any country in particular and should be passionately preserved. I do not think it is justifiable for any country to destroy such a rich bounty of nature just to extend the size of its towns and cities, or to increase the land available for farming and cultivation.

Forests are a natural habitat for many rare and sometimes endangered species of wild animals and birds. It is due to the unrestricted destruction of natural forests that many rare species of animals and birds have now almost become extinct in the world.

Some of the rarest of such species now exist only in the pages of science magazines and journals, and not in their natural habitat. In fact, forests can be termed as biological communities. It is a complex association of trees with other plants and animals that have evolved together over millions of years. Because of the unrestrained destruction of the forests, many unique and fascinating animals, such as the orangutan, the mountain gorilla, manatee, and exotic birds like the Puerto Rican parrot are threatened with near extinction. The destruction of tropical forests has also threatened the existence of migratory birds that sometimes journey more than 1000 miles from their summer breeding grounds in the north to their tropical winter nesting places in the south.

Forests also have tremendous economic and ecological value. Tropical forests especially, are home to some of the largest plant and animal genetic resources. It is stated that the forests of Puerto Rico contain more than 500 species of trees belonging to nearly 70 botanical families. One study has also suggested that tropical forests may contain as many as 25 million different kinds of plants and animals, most of which belong to the insect kingdom. They also abound in diversity of species, such as shrubs, herbs, mammals birds, reptiles, and amphibians.

Natural forests provide many valuable products like rubber, medicinal herbs, lumber, firewood, charcoal, and eatables like fruits and nuts. Some of the best-known drugs like quinine for the treatment of malaria are sourced from the tropical forests. Many plants from tropical forests like ferns, palms and orchids find use in gardens and homes as ornamental plants.

Perhaps the most important benefits of the natural forests pertain to their environmental aspects. Through the process of transpiration, the enormous number of plants and trees return huge amounts of water to the atmosphere, which helps to increase the humidity and rainfall. Also, through the process of photosynthesis, they help to greatly refine the atmosphere by drawing in the carbon dioxide and releasing oxygen. In this way trees also complement animals in the global environment. Mammals breathe in oxygen from the air and exhale carbon dioxide. Plants use the carbon dioxide in their growth process, store carbon in their woody tissues, and return oxygen to the atmosphere as a waste product. This is also known as the carbon cycle. The leaves of trees also act as filters to remove atmospheric pollutants from the air. By 'trapping' the carbon content they help to counteract the global 'greenhouse' effect. Their deep roots help to bind the soil together and thus prevent denudation of land. They also act as a brake on flash floods by helping to moderate the flow of the rushing waters.

They greatly help to maintain the ecological balance of a place. Mindless destruction of natural forests adversely impacts weather conditions and the pattern of rainfall over the concerned place. Trees act as a kind of environmental buffer for the local ecosystem. They help to mitigate extreme conditions of heat and cold, thus making life more comfortable and livable for the mammals.

Natural forests also provide tremendous tourist potential for the country where they are situated. Game reserves and wild life parks, which can be carved out of the forests, are a rich source of tourist attraction and thus bring economic prosperity to the country.

In view of such critical and manifold benefits, which accrue to mankind in general, the mindless destruction of forests should be forthwith stopped by the adoption of the most stringent measures by world governments. The survival of the natural forests can be said to be in the best interest of the efficient survival of the earthly species themselves.

Q3. Following the highest standards of ethics is the surest way to lasting success in business. Discuss the extent you agree or disagree with the opinion stated above. Support your views with reasons and/or examples from your own experience, observations, or reading.

A3. I am in complete and absolute agreement with this assertion. There is no better route to success in business than that of honesty, integrity and unstinted ethical behaviour.

There are many people who pursue the path of least resistance in business. This is the path of quick profits, insatiable profiteering, cheating on products and services and evasion of duties and taxes. To such unscrupulous businessmen, the customer is nothing more than the proverbial lamb and an expendable commodity in their quest for the fast buck. Fortunately, the life span of such businesses is comparatively short and uncertain. There is no dearth of such companies and business houses and examples abound in the market place. Everybody is aware of their identity and no names need be taken.

Glory, however, belongs only to those enterprises that follow the highest standards of ethics in their dealings with their customers, suppliers, and other business associates. To them, their customer is king. Success to them is not measured merely in terms of monetary profits, but in the satisfaction of their customers. They do not sell a product just to make a profit, but to fulfill the customer's need. Their motto is service, not gain. Gain is natural and inevitable but deemed to be incidental. They adhere to the highest standards of quality for their customers and the highest standards of safety for their workers. They work on the principle of low profits and higher turnover. If quality has ever been inadvertently compromised on a product or service, they are most happy to take back the defective product or compensate the customer suitably for the deficiency in service. Their rates are fixed uniform, and there is no favouritism or bias towards anyone. Their dealings are honest and straightforward and there is no cheating in weight or measure. Often their products carry official marks of quality.

Such businesses are an asset to the society that they serve. Customers are attracted to them because they follow the highest standards of ethics, and having bought their requirements from them, leave their premises with a smile of satisfaction on their faces: only to return happily another day.

Such enterprises alone enjoy lasting success in business. In course of time they become institutions by themselves. Who has not heard of a Bata for footwear, or of Ford or GM for motorcars, or of Lever for personal products – makers of products of excellence? Who has not heard of Prudential for insurance, or Thomas Cook for travel or Microsoft for software – providers of services of excellence?

Q4. Community patrolling is the best way to prevent crime. Discuss the extent you agree or disagree with the opinion stated above. Support your views with reasons and/or examples from your own experience, observations, or reading.

A4. I cannot vouch that community patrolling is the best way to prevent crime, though it certainly is one of most effective ways of combating crime in the neighbourhood.

The need for community patrolling generally arises when crime is on the rise in the neighbourhood, especially in the residential areas, and the local police do not have the required manpower to deal effectively with it. It is especially useful when there is a sudden spurt in thefts, burglaries, robberies, and other anti-social activities in a particular neighbourhood, or even the entire town or city. It is also useful during periods of political turmoil, communal clashes and civil unrest, when the law and order machinery is stretched to the limit and is thus unable to effectively help the people. In community patrolling, local residents and other volunteers organise themselves into small groups and take turns, often during the night, to move around the neighbourhood and keep vigil. Since they are familiar with the neighbourhood residents, they are easily able to spot strangers and other suspicious elements that might be waiting to create trouble. These volunteer groups usually function under the supervision of the local police, and are at times even accompanied by one or two constables. Community patrolling is also extremely helpful in dealing with cases of juvenile delinquency, eve-teasing, and other undesirable social behaviour. Based on the information and intelligence provided by the volunteers, the police can then act swiftly and efficiently to put down the menace of crime and arrest the wrongdoers. To that extent it is a very effective means of combating crime.

However, community patrolling does have its limitations. It cannot prevent or solve the more serious instances of crime like murders, rapes and kidnappings.

Community patrolling may also have its failings. It is quite possible that local goons and antisocial elements might themselves infiltrate into the volunteer groups and terrorise

17

the local residents and resort to extortion of money. Or, they might instigate the local police to act against innocent civilians by providing them with false information.

Thus, it can be surmised that though community patrolling is good for combating local crime, it does have its own limitations. The best way of preventing crime would undoubtedly be to strengthen the official law and order machinery by inducting officers of proven integrity, simulated sensitisation through on the job training of all ranks, weeding out the black sheep, and increasing the manpower to the desired levels. A strengthening of the intelligence networks and the judicial system would also help attain the desired results.

Q5. "Crime never pays," is the message in most movies, yet there is no dearth of crime in the world. Discuss what in your opinion are the reasons for crime in society and if movies have any role in it.

A5. Most people feel that the prevalence and rise of crime in the world is to a very great extent to be blamed on the excessive violence and abuse of all kind shown in films. Yet as the above statement proclaims, most films end with the message that "crime never pays". Why then is there so much of real crime in the world? Are movies really to be blamed, or are there other reasons as well? Let us examine the issue in more detail to arrive at a satisfactory answer.

Let us first consider issues other than films. Social scientists generally believe that the crime rate in society is largely linked to the socio-economic factors affecting different sections of the people. People who belong to the least privileged sections of society are more vulnerable to crime. Not just as perpetrators, but also as its victims. To understand the issue more clearly, we will have to broadly classify the varied forms of crime. In the first category, we may include such forms of relatively lesser crime as petty theft, larceny, pick pocketing and the like. These are generally confined to the lower strata of society and are usually the result of acute economic and social backwardness. In this category we can also include crimes related to juvenile delinquency, which are sometimes the result of acute poverty, and sometimes related to more serious social issues like divorce between the parents, neglect at home, drug and liquor abuse, and sometimes social boycott. Due to the absence of any moderating influence at home or outside, such individuals are easily motivated and inspired by scenes depicting crime in movies. They generally perceive themselves to be the wronged, rather than the wrongdoers, and tend to be inspired by the glorification of crime in some films.

In the second category, we may include the more serious crimes like dacoity, kidnapping, extortion, murder, and sexual abuse. While the first three in this category are usually carried out by organised gangs or hardened criminals, the last two are usually related to personal or social factors. Sexual abuse, though, can be sometimes linked to the portrayal of vulgarity and obscenity in films, which tend to arouse the carnal passions in man. But the perverted group – the homosexuals – have a vast network of their own constituting millions. They are not usually influenced by movies. In rare cases, it could be a revenge motive also. To the last category would belong the numerous instances of what are called white-collar crimes. These are, quite ironically committed by people belonging even to the upper strata of society, and include such cases as corporate and bank frauds, cheating, financial misappropriation, forgery and the like. Financial greed and the itch to get rich quickly is normally the motive for these types of offences and films, rather than being the cause of such crimes, may actually be based upon such real life instances.

From the above discussion, it would appear that while films may have some role in the proliferation of certain forms of crime, they cannot be said to be the sole or even the main cause. Otherwise every other person who comes out of a cinema hall would forthwith turn a criminal. Also, crime has existed even before the first movie ever hit the silver screen. At worst, some films may be said to exert a negative influence on those who are already vulnerable and inclined to wrongdoing. This would seem to answer the question raised in the issue that crime persists in society although most movies end with the message that crime does not pay.

Q6. Every business should ideally set aside some part of its profits; say 10%, to be spent on community welfare. Discuss the extent you agree or disagree with the opinion stated above. Support your views with reasons and/or examples from your own experience, observations, or reading.

A6. In an idealistic world, the idea to set aside about ten percent of a company's profits for community service is truly a laudable one and I am fully in agreement with it. Nonetheless, how far is it really practical? Let us consider both the aspects to reach a satisfactory answer.

First, the ideal. A company earns profits in the area where it operates and from the customers whom it serves. Is it then not fair that it should earmark a small portion of such profits to serve the community, which helps it to earn? The money could either be spent alone, or pooled together with similar contributions from other establishments, and spent jointly. The funds so generated could be usefully spent on providing better lighting in the area, building bus shelters, improving pavements, constructing and maintaining public parks, and on providing education and healthcare to the least privileged sections of the community. A part of the funds collected could also be buffer stocked to be donated in times of national calamities and natural disasters. This would not only win for the businesses the love and affection of the local community they serve, but also ensure

19

customer loyalty. In this way they could grow even further, and thereby generate even better funds for people's welfare.

Now, the reality. Companies don't always make profits. Sometimes they even make losses, especially in the initial years of operation. Much of the profits made in later years go to a great extent to recoup the losses of the earlier years. In such an eventuality, how are they to generate the required funds for community service? Secondly, companies are taxed on all their profit. This would substantially reduce the resources available for community service. The companies ought to utilise the tax exemption on donations for infrastructural development. Thirdly, in joint ventures, all the partners or stakeholders should agree to donate. In the event of dissent from some, the money cannot be donated.

Notwithstanding these hurdles, instances are not wanting where several big business houses spend substantial amounts of money from separate trusts formed for the purpose for adopting complete villages or townships, which are then suitably developed and maintained. Wells are dug and even irrigation facilities are provided to the farmers in the area. Schools are established for imparting free education to the underprivileged, and hospitals are built to provide healthcare to the needy, free of cost. Such companies not only earn the goodwill of their customers, but also the gratitude of the masses that they serve.

Q7. Greed and fear are the two emotions that drive human beings. Discuss the extent you agree or disagree with the opinion stated above. Support your views with reasons and/or examples from your own experience, observations, or reading.

A7. It is true that greed and fear are the two dominant emotions, which drive human beings hither and thither. Almost everyone suffers from greed. And almost everyone is haunted by fear. Let us explore these emotions in greater depth and comprehend their effect on people.

Greed is the tendency and desire to possess more, and more, and still more. There is virtually no end to greed. Greed, it is said, ends only with the greedy one. Greed is fuelled by the cravings of the mind. First, it is a craving for just pure simple subsistence. That achieved, it is a craving for the perceived essentials of life. Then for comforts, followed by luxuries. When nothing is left to buy, it is for power and fame. Each dimension of craving seamlessly merges into the next. And so the appetite for greed is vetted more and more. This despicable emotion is best exemplified in the foremost domain of speculation – the stock market. People trade in shares to make a quick buck. But do they really succeed in doing so? Not really. Because of greed, they never sell even when they have bought cheaper. They wait for the price to rise a little more, and when it has risen, they wait for it to rise still more. Till there is no more. The wise one takes his profits, while the greedy one takes only the losses. Fear is also cousin to greed. The same example will teach us more. Having bought in greed, they wait for the price of the share to rise so that they can quickly make their profit. But instead, it falls, and falls even further. Now they are afraid. No amount of reasoning will convince them. Friends tell them to hold some more. But they are scared and sell. Only to see the stock bounce fully back and soar much higher than the price at which they had bought. Oh, if only they had waited a little longer, they fume at themselves. But fear made them act. And loose.

Beware ye mortals! Fall not a victim to greed. Nor to fear. Remember, they are cousins and the one quickly follows the other.

Q8. Because of the availability of easy credit nowadays, people save too little and spend too much. Discuss the extent you agree or disagree with the opinion stated above. Support your views with reasons and/or examples from your own experience, observations, or reading.

A8. This statement, unfortunately, reflects the reality of the times. This is a malaise afflicting most sections of the society, especially the urban middle classes. It is also a symptom of the gross materialism that pervades modern society. The heightened consumerism, fanned by an explosive growth of a diverse range of products and services for the people, and further fuelled by the availability of easy credit in the marketplace has turned this phenomenon into a veritable monster, which constantly consumes the earnings of the households, leaving them with little or no savings.

Let us try and analyze each of these factors individually in order to measure the impact of this new trend on the people.

The first factor is the heightened consumerism in society. Because of high rates of growth in some countries, per capita income levels have risen, resulting in more purchasing power with the people. This has created an insatiable desire in the people to possess all types of comforts and luxuries that money can buy. It has resulted in a desire to own more and more products and services. Possession of the latest gadgets lure then into mega spending. Because of the impact of globalisation, these trends do not remain confined to any one country, but spread out far and wide across the continents. The second factor is the actual availability of all types of goods and services. Increased industrialisation and the rapid technological advances made in recent times have seen an explosive growth in the availability of a truly diverse range of goods and services in the marketplace which beckon enticingly to the people, from the attractively laid out shop shelves and windows. Online shopping has also become the latest fad. Igniting this urge to possess is the easy availability of credit, which constitutes the third and the last factor.

Realising the mismatch between the people's urge to purchase a wide variety of products and services flooding the marketplace on the one hand and the constraint of their income on the other, financial institutions, like banks and other consumer lending agencies, sensing the unlimited opportunities open to them, have unleashed a barrage of lending options in the market, inducing the people to buy as if there was no tomorrow. Thus, we see the spectacle of people borrowing to build houses, buy expensive cars, jewels, all kinds of home products, go on foreign vacations, and in short indulge their fancies in every conceivable way. This has, over a period of time, made them slaves to the borrowing habit and victim to the mounting debts and never ending installments. Many a time they have to borrow afresh to settle their old dues. And so the vicious cycle goes on. In this mad merry-go-round of consumers chasing credit and then the creditors chasing them, the biggest casualty has been the all-important savings, which the households once enjoyed.

Alas! today there is very little saving, only much more spending.

Q9. "The heart rules over the head." Advertising agencies seem to be guided only by this dictum, when they design advertisements for the people. What do you think is the meaning of this dictum, and discuss to what extent you agree or disagree.

A9. Good advertising, it is said, can help sell bad products! And good advertisements always appeal straight to the heart, never to the head. Shrewd advertisement managers have well understood the meaning of the dictum, "The heart rules over the head." In simple parlance, this refers to those persons who are guided in their decisions only by their emotions, and not by their reason. Such simple folk are the biggest target audience of crafty executives of ad agencies.

Many people act only upon impulse. They also buy on impulse. Later they might realise that they had really no good reason to buy, except that they just felt like buying! Perhaps they had seen someone use the product before. But who? And where? Yes, now they remember! It was their favourite movie hero who they had seen bragging about the product, just a few days ago, on their television screen. This is the story of the maneuvering skills of the advertisement gurus. And how they make their products succeed. Let us view a few examples.

How often not has a doting mother of a two-year-old girl rushed to the nearest store to buy a jar of the latest baby food in the market, after hearing its virtues being extolled by a happy looking mother, cuddling her chubby faced young child close to her? How often not has a middle-aged woman picked up her phone to forthwith place an order for a new weight-reduction gadget displayed on the television in her room, by a charmingly slim lady, who somehow miraculously lost 15 pounds in just 15 days! And how often not has a teenager bought an expensive watch for her heartthrob on his birthday, after a pretty girl announced on TV that it was the best gift to give to a boyfriend. And how often not has a once adamant husband quickly called in an insurance agent to buy an insurance policy on his life, after he saw the pathetic scene of a woman, surrounded by her little children, sobbing uncontrollably after learning that her husband, the sole breadwinner in the family had suddenly died in a road accident? .

These are only a few examples of how effective the medium of advertisement has proved to be in reaching out to people, and their hearts. It has been said that the way to a man's heart is through his stomach. It is equally true that the way to a customer's wallet is through his heart! Trust the ad man to do just that!

Q10. Machines are increasingly replacing men in the workplace. This will lead to zero-defect products and error-free services. Discuss the extent you agree or disagree with the opinion stated above. Support your views with reasons and/ or examples from your own experience, observations, or reading.

A10. It is a fact that machines are increasingly replacing men in the workplace. But it will be more precise to say that machines are actually complementing men in the workplace. They can never ever replace men completely. Will this lead to zero-defect products and error-free services for people? Not entirely. After all even machines are subject to occasional breakdowns (like humans!), and computers arguably work only on artificial intelligence!

It is well known that some of the leading products made in the developed countries like Japan are manufactured using the most technologically advanced machines and processes. In fact, most of the assembly lines are operated with the help of robots. Yet, can we say that every car that rolls out of Japan, or the hi-tech gadgetry produced there will never have even a single defect? Not so long ago there was the case of a leading car tyre manufacturer in the world, who had to call back the entire stock of car tyres in the market, because they were found to have caused several accidents, due to an inherent defect in them. Then again, take the case of the NASA space shuttle, which exploded into a horrendous ball of flame in the recent past, on its return trip, sending its entire crew hurtling to its fiery grave. This colossal tragedy was reportedly caused by a technical fault in the outer body of the spaceship, which caused the temperatures to soar to unsustainable levels. Will we still swear that machines can help create zero-defect products?

As for services, the advent of high-grade computers have definitely helped to reduce to almost negligible levels, the scope for serious errors, which would otherwise be associated with the human hand. Thus, millions of secure and virtually error-free transactions take place in the world everyday through the use of Internet technology in several diverse sectors like banking, insurance, travel, stock and commodity exchanges, and even on-line shopping. The use of advanced computer technologies and processes in modern passenger and defense aircraft is well known. The use of supercomputers in nuclear technology and other critical areas is also widely recognised.

All these have made the wired and the wireless world much safer, though not cent percent safe. There is always scope for the unexpected glitch, the unforeseen factor. This is proved by the fact that even the best-designed airliners sometimes crash (Concord), and the most advanced spacecraft sometime fail to return their crew members to earth.

Q11. In order to save on salaries, companies are increasingly hiring younger people in the age group of 20 to 25. Discuss to what extent you agree or disagree with the above. Give reasons and/or examples from your own experience, observations or reading.

A11. While I do agree that companies are increasingly hiring younger people in the age group of 20 to 25, I don't really think that the prime motive is to save on salaries, by offering them lower pay packets. Nonetheless, this benefit may accrue to the companies, though it is largely incidental. What then has moved the companies to hire younger staff? Let us try and look for the reasons.

Today we are living in a very dynamic world, a world where technologies change by the hour. Old processes and techniques become increasingly obsolete and newer ones quickly take their place. In this world of fast change, only the younger generation will be bold and swift enough to adapt to the newer trends and the emerging technologies. Youngsters are more technology-savvy than their older counterparts. This is natural because they have grown up in the midst of high speed computers and mobile protocols. Fast paced action is part of their life statement.

The corporate sector has developed a globalised vision. They have to or they will perish. The increasing thrust towards adoption and assimilation of the latest technologies has made the increased hiring of younger people imperative.

Another factor in their favour is the new culture of business outsourcing and the increased need for companies, especially those in the service sector, to establish their own call centers. Business outsourcing effectively means that the older and higher paid staff are relieved of their jobs in the company back offices, and the work outsourced to other agencies, many a time in different countries, who then recruit the younger persons, generally in their early twenties to do the work. Ditto is the case with call-centers. It must be admitted that in this type of work migration, many a times across seamless borders, saving on staff salaries are a prime consideration. This type of work is routine in nature, and does not need any specialised skills. And the younger people with their greater stamina and enthusiasm fit the bill perfectly. Further, the work does call for working in shifts, both day and night. The strenuous nature of this exercise then makes the younger people a natural choice.

Q12. Societies that do not respect and honour their women can never ever make progress. Discuss to what extent you agree or disagree with the above. Give reasons and/or examples from your own experience, observations or reading.

A12. It is said that behind every successful man is a woman. It can be said with even more truth and conviction that behind every successful country is the respect, honour, and chivalry shown to its women.

What is it that distinguishes developed countries from the undeveloped? Economic progress achieved? No. High standards of living attained? No, again. The answer lies in the way society treats its weaker members: its womenfolk. No society that brutalises its women can be said to have become even civilised, leave alone developed.

The desire to dominate over others is to be construed as a sign of weakness, not strength. The desire to brutalise another is beastly. The urge to inflict injury on a fellow-human is certainly inhuman. How much more despicable would be to inflict these abuses on a weak and helpless woman? Yet, this is the fate of women in several male-dominated societies even today. Male domination and chauvinism is generally perpetuated in the name of religion and tradition. Women normally have no rights in certain societies. Not even the right to education, or the right to free movement. Women are not even allowed to take up employment. All their fundamental rights, social, economic, and even political are curtailed. Their domination is complete and unambiguous.

Why can such societies or such countries make no progress? Why are they doomed to eternal failure? The reasons are obvious. They are denied the advantage of the collective wisdom and intelligence of their entire womenfolk. They are denied the moderating influence of women in the midst of male strife. They are denied the advantages of employing women in their workplaces. By segregating women from the mainstream of society, they have grievously split their body politic into two. By not educating their women, they are also denying their own children the opportunity of good parenting. Today women are the torchbearers in the more enlightened societies of the world. They have proved to be able administrators, mature statespersons, enlightened educationists, savvy executives, and above all, the most efficient homemakers. While Margaret Thatcher, Indira Gandhi, and several other women personalities symbolised women power in world politics and statesmanship, the legendary Florence Nightingale and the more recent Nobel Laureate, Mother Teresa exemplified the nobility of purpose in their unstinted and untiring service of suffering humanity. They represented the sublime face of womanhood, its inclination towards selfless service and sacrifice.

Woman is God's gift to man. Disrespecting, dishonouring, and demonising her would mean inviting the wrath of God Himself. God did create man, but it was woman who gave him birth. Man would do well to remember that, lest he preside over his own annihilation.

Q13. A degree may help a person get a job, but not promotion. Discuss to what extent you agree or disagree with the above. Give reasons and/or examples from your own experience, observations or reading.

A13. This is absolutely true. Everyone is anxious to get a college degree, as this is considered to be the only passport to a good job. But how far can a person travel with it? Let us find out.

In most countries a college degree is a prised possession. People work hard to earn one. The burning of the midnight oil, the stress and strain of the examinations, and the tension of waiting for the final results is finally rewarded in the form of the prized degree. In some countries, degrees are also sometimes unfortunately sold for a price.

However, the degree is no guarantee to promotion. For that, one has to surely prove himself. Entry into the job has provided him the opportunity to prove his true worth. He will need to work hard and with dedication. He will need to fully exercise the skills, which he learnt in the course of his education. He will have to exhibit his team spirit and work well with his colleagues. He will also need to respect his seniors and show that he values their advice and suggestions. He will need to serve the customers and clients with diligence and sincerity. He will have to learn the time-management skills to adhere to the tight schedule of deadlines. He will have to tender his suggestions to his superiors with a sense of humility. In short he will have to be politeness personified.

After all this, if he is lucky to get a promotion, he needs to silently bow his head in gratitude to god, and say a loud, "Thank you," to his boss.

Q14. Governments should spend their resources on improving food, drinking water, power, education, healthcare, and housing for the people rather than waste them on space exploration and the like. Discuss to what extent you agree or disagree with the above. Give reasons and/or examples from your own experience, observations or reading.

A14. It is many, many, years since man first set foot on the moon. But that conquest stirred his appetite greatly, and set him firmly on the course of further expeditions into the unknown frontiers of space. And so it continues to this day. But has man stopped to ponder? Have governments paused to calculate the incredibly astronomical sums of money that they spend to put their spacecraft into space. Have they ever wondered if the results obtained have justified the huge expense incurred? Is life on this planet where we humans live any better of for all the effort and money invested? How will the discovery of some strange gasses or some unknown rocky substances on a faraway planet change the fortunes of this world? Will man ever be able to make his home on Mars?

These are profound questions that beg answers, and governments who indulge in this ultimate luxury of space travel at the cost of funds collected from the harried taxpayer are bound to provide the answers.

Have governments ever paused to think about the manifold benefits that the inhabitants of this planet could derive if the resources so easily squandered on space exploration, are instead utilised for providing more food, drinking water, power, education and health care for the millions of underprivileged citizens of this world. These would be tangible and visible benefits indeed, unlike the supposed and presumed benefits that might one day accrue to the privileged few belonging to the scientific community of the world.

Do the governments know that millions of people across the world live on no more than one meal a day, and sometimes go to sleep even without that, for want of enough food to eat? Do they know that innumerable people fall seriously ill and even die due to lack of proper drinking water in several countries? Do they know that children cannot study after dusk for want of electricity in villages? Do they know that more than half of the world's population is mired in illiteracy? Do they know that hundreds of famished and undernourished children and aged persons die every day because of inadequate health care?

I wish they do, for then perhaps their conscience will be stirred enough to force them to spend those precious funds on the poor and hapless people of this world, rather than on fanciful fantasies of another faraway world.

Q15. The human mind tries to find complex solutions to simple problems. Discuss the extent to which you agree or disagree.

A15. Perhaps it is part of human nature to be complex. Perhaps it is considered more intellectual or fashionable to be so. Perhaps we feel that it is shameful to be simple. But the plain simple fact is that we like to be complex, or more rightly complexed!

Why has man tied himself into so many knots? Why has he burdened himself with so many complexities in life? He is like a beast carrying a heavy burden on his back.

27

Why can't man be just simple? Then his problems also would appear simple to him, and the solutions even simpler. Perhaps it is the fault of the human mind. It tries to make trifles look crucial. It tries to perceive a problem, where perhaps none exists. It tries to make mountains out of molehills. If there are really no problems, then the mind tries its best to create them. How often have we not heard a person exclaim: "I'm so bored, that's the problem!"

It would not be an exaggeration to say that most problems are man-made. First the mind tends to create the problems, and then begins to visualise complex solutions to them. Take the simplest fact of life. We all eat food. Everyone does. But we turn this simple fact also into a complex problem. "Is the food healthy?" "How many calories does my meal contain?" "I shouldn't be eating so much of fatty foods." "I don't like my milk to be so sweet." "I like my coffee a little bitter." "I have to cut down on my food to reduce my weight." And so on and so forth. What a fuss we make over trivial things. We forget that there are innumerable people in this world who starve to death in exigent situations, but have none to eat.

Looks are important to all. Ageing is a natural phenomenon, and with the progression of years, the skin tends to get slightly wrinkled and the body begins to put on some flab. A 'minor problem' of ageing, no doubt. But our reaction is most complex indeed. We rush to the best and most expensive plastic surgeon and happily undergo the most complex and perhaps painful procedures to reverse the ageing process. Many others go under the surgeon's scalpel just to make their little nose look a little bit more cute, or to narrow down the voluminous posterior. These are all examples of 'complex' solutions to simple 'problems'.

The weather is a natural phenomenon, and we all know that it keeps changing. No 'problem' there really. But look at the fretting and fuming that follow when the mercury changes a few degrees. Clothing is a relatively 'minor problem'. But what intense 'complexities' are involved in designing a dress to perfection. Otherwise there would be a real problem, indeed! Sleep is such a natural occurrence. Yet, how much we complain about the 'problem' of insomnia? We have to go to doctors to find out why we are not able to sleep, and pop pills at night so that we do. How many people in this world have to actually forego enough sleep, so that they can keep the home fires burning?

If only we learn to count our blessings daily, we would be free of all problems and their complex solutions.

Q16. Some people feel that with the advent of Internet and television, books have greatly lost their relevance. Discuss to what extent you agree or disagree with the above. Give reasons and/or examples from your own experience, observations or reading.

A16. Though the advent of Internet and television have heralded the era of electronic communication, it is not entirely correct to say that books have greatly lost their relevance. After all everything has its own place under the sun. So do the electronic media and the physical books. At best, Internet and television could be said to have supplemented the reading habit, not replaced or displaced it.

Having emphasised the importance of both, let us try and understand to what extent the system of electronic communication has supplemented the reading of books. We can get the true picture only if we segment books into their respective categories, and see which category of books have steadfastly held their ground, and which category have surrendered some of their importance to the electronic mode.

In the first category, fall books dealing with the academic curriculum of various educational institutions, including schools and colleges. These have firmly held their ground and are absolutely irreplaceable. Students still need to buy the books prescribed by their schools and colleges, and carry them to their classes for learning. No amount of computerisation in the classrooms can change this reality. However, what is relevant is that the Internet provides a student with a virtually inexhaustible wealth of reference material, and factual data, which he can readily access by surfing the net. In this way he can greatly enhance his knowledge, without leaving the comfort of his classroom or home. Thus he saves time and also money, which would have been otherwise spent in purchasing the reference books. Not only that, he has access to a much wider pool of knowledge and resources, virtually free of cost, just at the click of a mouse, than he would have, were he to depend on books alone.

In the second category, we can include all types of general educational books like dictionaries, thesauruses, and the like. The usage of these books would have been affected to a minor extent, with the uploading of some of their content on the Internet portals. Other books dealing with a diverse range of subjects like linguistics, sciences, mathematics, history, geography, art, cookery, hobbies and the like, written by different authors would hardly be affected in any way. This is more than evident from the robust sales at the book counters.

In the third category, would fall all category of books dealing with fiction. These books being a source of ready companionship for the frequent traveler as well as the home bird, their position is unassailable.

From the above discussion, it is amply clear that while Internet and television provide valuable knowledge resources, as well as recreational features, at relatively much lower costs, books as the prime source of knowledge and joy will continue to prevail.

Q17. Governments should do away with censoring of films and instead leave this function to be performed by an independent panel of film producers. Discuss to what extent you agree or disagree with the above. Give reasons and/or examples from your own experience, observations or reading.

A17. Movies have in recent times become highly maligned as a medium of entertainment. They have been criticised by many people, for portraying excessive scenes of crime and violence, as well as displaying obscenity and vulgarity; thereby seriously undermining the moral fiber of society. Several people believe that movies have been directly responsible for the rising crime graph in countries, and hence stringent measures need to be taken by the government to curb their debasing influence on society in general. Governments have responded to this criticism by setting up film censor boards, comprising of eminent members from a wide spectrum of society, including representatives of the government, so as to view the films before their release and suggest cuts and changes in whatever scenes are perceived to be objectionable. This is the status quo. Whether the suggestion that these government sponsored censor boards should be replaced with a panel of independent producers to perform this function is justified or not is a highly debatable one. Much would depend on which side of the fence one views this recommendation from – the peoples' side or the filmmakers' side.

That the suggestion would prove more convenient to the filmmakers is quite obvious. The censor board, no doubt, is the ultimate nightmare of any film producer, and which moviemaker would not be pleased if his film were to be viewed by none other than a panel consisting of members of his own fraternity? After all, who can understand and empathise with the problems and compulsions of a film producer better than another fellow film producer? Surely, the fellow producers would agree that movie making is no child's play after all. It is common knowledge that huge resources are invested in the making of a movie, to provide the kind of ingredients that the box office demands. It has to be an assortment of thrills, no doubt. Violence, crime, sex abuse, double-meaning songs, semi-nude scenes, and perhaps gay behaviour are the heady ingredients, which have to be somehow integrated with a wafer-thin story line to pass off for an eminently viewable movie. So what, if some self-appointed moralists spew venom? Surely, movies are made for the masses, not for the select few, who pretend to be the conscience-keepers of society? And after all, are they not just portraying in their films the reality that actually exists outside the movie theaters? And, what is wrong with nudity and sex? Don't they constitute normal human behaviour?

The arguments would be endless. After all, it's their business, and their fortunes at stake. But society also has a stake, and a much bigger one – in its own survival, and a survival of its cherished values. This then makes it imperative that the dream peddlers are

30

not allowed to completely tarnish the moral fiber of society, or to muddy the minds of the young, who throng to watch their movies.

Government sponsored censor boards owe it to society to ensure this and much more.

Q18. In view of the rising prices and demand for oil, countries should discourage the production of large and luxury cars, which consume unnecessary fuel. Discuss to what extent you agree or disagree with the above. Give reasons and/or examples from your own experience, observations or reading.

A18. It is said that oil reserves cannot last forever. However, at the present rate of consumption, fuel reserves may exhaust themselves sooner than later. Hence, great circumspection is called for in the consumption of fuel. The prices of oil have been steadily climbing ever since the first Iraq war and have now reached historic levels. Ironically enough, this has done nothing to lower the demand for oil. On the contrary, the level of demand keeps rising. This is a contradictory situation, and could seriously jeopardise the world economy. Obviously, the consumer is not deterred by the unusually high price of oil. The explosive rate of industrial growth taking place in the developing countries, especially the two most populated nations and the fastest growing economies of the world, India and China, have ensured that the demand for oil continues to be at a peak.

What can countries all over do to reverse this dangerous escalation in the price and demand for oil? For a start, they should ensure that there is a halt to the gratuitous and superfluous consumption of the precious commodity. Oil, quite literally, keeps the wheels of the economy moving. The transport sector is perhaps the biggest consumer of oil. If there has to be any meaningful reduction in the use of oil, then the governments have to ensure that any unnecessary and wasteful consumption in this sector has to be forthwith eliminated. Freebies in the govt. sector also need to be curtailed.

It is in this context that the suggestion for governmental discouragement for the production of Sedan; luxury cars assumes importance. These symbols of luxury and fame are almost exclusively used by the rich, to pamper their bloated egos, and make no real economic or social sense. They are a total misnomer in today's times and serve no useful purpose except to guzzle excessive quantities of valuable fuel. As it is futile to wish that any amount of taxes and duties imposed would dent their sale, countries would be well advised to altogether ban their production and sale. The production facilities thus rendered vacuous could be gainfully employed to manufacture smaller and more fuel-efficient cars for the use of the common man. This will not only achieve a welcome, though limited, reduction in the use of oil, but also underline the social overtones of the action.

Q19. Success means to be able to live life according to one's own convictions. Do you agree or disagree. If yes, state why; if not, discuss what constitutes success according to you. Support your views with reasons and/or examples drawn from your own experiences, observations or readings.

A19. Success is a relative concept. It has always to be measured against something else. There is no uniform yardstick of success for all people and for all times. What may constitute success to one may be equivalent to failure to another. Similarly what qualifies for success today may be a sign of failure tomorrow. Therefore it is futile to assert that success means that one should be able to live life according to one's own convictions. Who decides if such convictions are right or wrong? Again, they have to be measured against something else-perhaps social values and norms. This again might differ from society to society and country to country. Let us examine the matter in depth.

Some people believe that success is to be measured in terms of money. A person is generally considered successful if he is wealthy and has done well in his business or profession. But what is the quantum of money and wealth that a person should possess to qualify for the word 'successful'? Should it be the possession of an apartment or a house, or the ownership of a scooter or a motorcar? Should it be related to the amount of his fixed deposits in bank, or the furniture and fittings in his house? Should the bungalow owner be called more successful than the owner of an apartment? After all, the bungalow might have been inherited and the flat purchased on loan from the bank. Can we say that the owner of a motorcar is more successful than the owner of a two-wheeler? If the answer is yes, then how do we rate the motorcar owner to another person who has two motorcars? Similarly, can we link success to the position one holds in his office? We can theorise that the manager is more successful than the clerk, thereby implying that the clerk is not a successful person. But can we not consider the clerk to be more successful than the office peon?

Some people rate success on the social scale. They link it to a person's private life. Some may consider him successful if he is married and settled. Some may consider him successful if he has managed to continue to remain married for 10 years or more.

Yet others may consider him successful if he is a social hit and is often invited to the local parties. The sports club may consider him successful if he is a good badminton player.

Again, what constitutes success at one period of time may not be so considered at some other period of time. Hence a survival rate of 70% or more may have been considered as a sign of success in heart surgeries conducted half a century ago, while a success rate of anything lesser than 98% may be considered to be an indication of failure today.

This reiterates the view that success is a relative concept. It is relative to so many factors, not just one. Hence a person who is considered to be extremely successful in his business may be considered to be a miserable failure in his personal life. There is really no fixed definition of success.

Viewed from this perspective, it appears very naïve to classify success on the basis of one's own convictions and his ability to live life according to them. What if his convictions are totally flawed? After all, there are many people in the world with 'jihadi' convictions. They not only swear fanatically by their own convictions, but also would happily go about killing and maiming other people who won't. Is this then to be construed as a sign of great success?

At one time winning wars was considered to be a sure sign of success. A few decades later, today, winning peace is considered as a bigger sign of success.

Q20. Internet provides a very useful tool for communication, but it is also susceptible to misuse. Discuss to what extent you agree or disagree, and give reasons/ and or examples.

A20. There is much truth in this statement. The advent of Internet has changed the face of the information technology and revolutionised the world of communication. Gone are the days of writing letters and waiting for the arrival of the local postman. Gone are the days of inordinate delay and of missing mail. Today, messages from any part of the globe are received in a trice and replies sent in a twinkling! Not only the written word, but also pictures and images can be flashed across the continents in a jiffy. People use the Internet to indulge in lengthy personal chats, and businessmen to conduct extended negotiations. Internet is also effectively used to transmit technical advice from specialist doctors in one part of the globe to hospitals and health centers in another. Major surgeries are performed in this fashion by doctors, with the help and coordination of medical experts sitting thousands of miles away, watching the procedures on their Internet screen and communicating the required instructions to their counterparts.

It is extremely regrettable that such a highly convenient and effective medium of modern communication has also seen much misuse since its inception. The transmitting of obscene and pornographic material through dubious websites is a cause for serious concern. Another area of misuse is the mushrooming of so-called "friendship sites" and chat rooms of doubtful nature, which tend to lure the young and vulnerable. Some of them claiming to provide "dating services" are no more than a cover for flesh trade and prostitution. These are some of the grey areas that need to be seriously probed by the law enforcement authorities, lest they lead to tragic consequences for those unfortunate few who are prepared to bite the bait. Children, being particularly vulnerable, need to be properly protected from the manipulations and machinations of the faceless monsters sitting across the other end of the line and functioning under fictitious identities. Internet, being the cutting edge of information and communications technology, spreads seamlessly across the international frontiers. This makes it imperative for world governments to act decisively and cohesively to take on the challenge of cyber crime and nab these neo-criminals hiding behind encrypted firewalls. Stringent cyber laws need to be framed for the hackers who enter the private domain through unauthorised access to data. These cyber walls need to be effectively dismantled and smashed in order to catch not only the peddlers of indecency and vulgarity, but also the wily authors of devious computer viruses, which cause immense harm to the computer systems across the globe, and lead to incalculable losses to their users.

Q21. Parents and teachers should focus only on the positive traits in children and ignore the negative ones. Discuss to what extent you agree or disagree with the above. Give reasons and/or examples from your own experience, observations or reading.

A21. Parents and teachers have an onerous role to play in shaping the destiny of the children. Children are the most precious assets of any country as they are its future citizens, and a country is only as good as its citizens. Hence, a great deal of care and circumspection has to be invested in the proper training and upbringing of the children.

Children being very young are highly impressionable and susceptible to proper molding. These two very important characteristics in children have to be leveraged to the maximum by the parents and teachers in order to develop proper values and inculcate the right behaviour in the young ones.

It is imperative that in the initial formative years, children have to be imbued with a sense of right and wrong. While every effort should be made to encourage and develop the positive traits in the young ones, care should also be taken to gently loosen the strands of the negative ones. A child, like everyone else in the world, is a bundle of both, positive and negative tendencies. A child, being highly impressionable, is liable to quickly imbibe both from his external environment. In course of time, these tendencies metamorphose into habits, both good and bad, and from these character is formed. As the individual begins to indulge in his habits, they become part and parcel of his nature, from which he will find it very hard to disengage at a later period.

This is why it is absolutely vital for parents and teachers to observe a child, closely and regularly, and monitor his mind, so as to be able to sift the positive traits from the negative. While the child should be praised and patted for the good, it would be a mistake to totally ignore the negative ones. Some people imagine that the bad qualities will go away by themselves as the child grows up and himself realises their worthlessness. But this may only prove to be illusionary thinking and a fond hope. It is possible that the negative traits may slip into the subconscious and gradually reawaken and resurface at a later date. Hence, every effort should be made by the parents and teachers to gently and lovingly wean the young one away from the clasp of the negative traits. If they fail to do this, then both would be failing in their duty not only to the young minds but also to themselves, as well as to their country.

Q22. Criticism is a virtue, because it is only when other people criticise us that we become aware of our own weaknesses. Discuss to what extent you agree or disagree with the above. Give reasons and/or examples from your own experience, observations or reading.

A22. I fully share the view expressed above. All people can criticise, but few can themselves face criticism. Everyone loves to criticise others, but himself wishes to be adored and praised. Everyone likes to believe that others can be wrong, but he alone is infallible. Others can make mistakes, but he cannot. Others are wicked, while he alone is a paragon of virtue.

However, a wise one will never shun criticism when it comes his way. He will listen to it attentively and in silence, and even thank the critic. He will then introspect deeply to see where his failings lie. And having discovered his shortcomings, will hasten to remove them. In this way he reforms himself. And redeems his soul.

Human nature is very frail. It is also very weak. We are all victims of the many failings of the mind. Ego rules the roost. Other vices like anger, jealousy, envy, covetousness, greed, pride, and attachment follow closely behind. Can anyone in this world truly claim that he is not a victim of these failings? Much as we know we are, we don't like to be told about our faults. We feel deeply aggrieved even if our parents and teachers point them out to us. We flare up instantly in anger. This itself is the biggest sign of our failings. If we will refuse to listen, how will we know? If a patient will not go to a doctor, he will never know if he is suffering from some unknown disease. Again, if he will flare up in anger at being told of his illness, how will he submit to a cure?

Virtue lies in accepting criticism with grace. We should treat the critic as our best friend, for it is only through his criticism that we will become aware of our latent faults. The critic need not always be a stranger. He can even be our friend, and possibly our truest friend. While false friends will deceive with their flattery or curry favour with their praise, only the true friend who really cares and has our utmost welfare at his heart will risk our displeasure by telling us the truth, howsoever unpalatable it may be to us. Many a time we are saved from serious situations through the sobering words of a well-meaning critic.

We all live in darkness as far as our faults are concerned. Many a time we actually mistake them for virtues. We are so deceived by them, that often we proudly flaunt them before others and display them as if they are our greatest assets. In normal light, we never see the dust in the room. But when sunlight enters, we clearly see the suspended particles in its beam.

Criticism is that beam of truth, which can show us our faults. It is also the torch, which can dispel the darkness in our mind and show us the light. It is to be considered as the biggest of virtues, and the one who criticises our best friend and truest guide.

Q23. No amount of laws can alter the way individuals think and act. Hence it is best to let people do what they want and learn through their own experience. Discuss to what extent you agree or disagree with the above. Give reasons and/or examples from your own experience, observations or reading.

A23. This is rather a dangerous proposition. It is suggested that people should be free to think and act as they wish, while the law should conveniently be kept aside. If implemented, it is sure to sound the death knell of civilised society and all that it stands for. It will be a return to the dark ages and the law of the jungle.

History does not encourage us to believe that people will always learn from their past mistakes. Otherwise, the bloody and violent wars, which inflicted so much death and devastation, and brought such a trail of suffering in their wake, would not be fought again and again. Also, the thief, who is caught stealing and sent to jail, would never steal again.

We have to confess that we do not live in an idealistic world, howsoever much we might wish it to be so. It is a hard and unforgiving world. It takes all kinds to make up the world. This is the place of duality. Good co-exists with the bad, night with day, and virtue with vice. If every individual were allowed to think and act just as he wished, without any let up or hindrance, then we would only unleash a multitude of raw passions in the world, which might denigrate us to the level of the denizens of the jungle. It is much easier to fall than it is to climb. It is much easier to be sinful than to be virtuous. It is futile to expect that all those who are either good or law abiding, are doing so purely out of choice. It is more likely due to the fear of the law.

A fallout of the culture of gross materialism is the increasing inclination of people to indulge in every conceivable whim and fancy. An offshoot of today's freer society is the strident demand from individuals for more and more of unfettered freedom in every conceivable walk of life. Everybody would like to act just as they wish without the restraining hand of society. This expression of unbridled individuality is nothing but a call for rights without responsibility. This is the thought process that bred the hippy culture

36

many years ago. Young people who were at loggerheads with organised civil society formed small groups to live the way they wanted. Those who sought an escape from life and its responsibilities were happy to join this 'brotherhood'. Their 'freedom' consisted of unrestrained indulgence in the passions. Their 'nirvana' was induced through the use of drugs like marijuana and brown sugar. Can civil society condone excesses such as these in the name of unmitigated individual freedom? Can it allow its members to willingly sink to the depths of depravity and then happily return to its fold after having undergone these 'illuminating' experiences? An extension of the same principle of uninhibited individuality is now becoming more visible in some of the more permissive societies in the world through the shrill demand to legalise gay marriages. Those who vociferously propagate that every person should be left free to act in any manner of his choosing, fail to realise that an individual is but a part of the larger society, and all his actions will ultimately rebound hard on the society itself.

Many a time, it also happens that the victim of one's wrongdoing is none other than the concerned person himself. Left unrestrained, even the best man might, inadvertently or otherwise, do something, which he may have to live to repent. A man cannot opt to take his own life, even though he may claim it to be his own. The law has to step in to prevent him from doing so, or he gets hoist with one's own Petard. Laws have been passed to discourage smoking, in the hope that the smoker would be saved. Similarly, to save the addicts from certain death, drugs have been banned, and peddlers given the harshest punishment, including the death penalty. Advertisements propagating liquour have been made illegal in many countries, and underage individuals prohibited from visiting bars serving alcoholic drinks. Again, laws have to be enacted to force the motorcyclists to wear helmets to save them from life threatening skull injuries, and drivers of motorcars have to be forced to wear their seat belts. Laws have to be enacted to protect the rights of the mother and the unborn or minor child in cases of an early divorce. The list is almost endless. It is almost as if people have to be forced to act in a way that keeps them out of harm's way. Hence, to suggest that the law allow people to think and act as they wish would be tantamount to saying that the mother give a lighted match to her child so that she can burn herself, and then perhaps learn from her bitter experience.

It is possible that some day in the distant future man might grow in stature, mentally and morally, and evolve to a degree where he would act only for the good of all, including himself. This would happen when he has totally subjugated his baser desires and ignoble instincts. Then, and only then, would laws become unnecessary and redundant. Till such time, society will have to learn to live with laws, and individuals with forced restraint.

Q24. People hold irrational and superstitious beliefs because science has not provided them with alternate rational explanations. Discuss to what extent this is true.

A24. Belief in superstition is as old as the creation itself. People have always believed in superstition, and will ever continue to do so. What is superstition and why do people religiously believe in it? Let us analyze.

Science has provided rational answers to most of the phenomena occurring in the universe. It has been able to decipher the physical laws, which govern this creation. It has understood and analyzed the composition of matter in its minutest detail. It has been successful in splitting the atom. It has effectively probed the genetic structure of living creatures and even succeeded in creating clones. Yet, there are some areas, which have remained inaccessible even to science. These belong to the realm of the metaphysical.

Take mind for instance. We are all aware of our own mind and even swear to ourselves that it is superior to that of others! But have we ever seen it? Most people confuse the mind with the brain. Yet we know it is not true. Doctors talk of only brain surgeries, never of mind surgeries. When the skull is dissected, the organ that reveals itself is the brain, not the mind.

Brain, is no doubt the thinking center of the body. Everybody acknowledges that. Yet it does not think by itself. Thinking is the function of the mind. In other words, mind functions through the physical brain. When we say that, "My mind tells me to do this or that," we are subconsciously acknowledging the presence of the mind. Yet, we know very little about the mind or its composition. No doctor has ever succeeded in discovering or dissecting the human mind. There is nothing strange, though. We are all aware of the presence of electricity in a live wire though we never ever see it. We know that the wire is only the medium of carriage or transmission, but the lethal current is something else. This is also the case with the mind. Mind does exist, but on a different plane, which is not physical. Being subtle, this plane is not visible to the physical eyes. Hence it is that science has not been able to probe the mysteries of this plane, because man does not have the superior faculties to conduct such an inquiry.

Man is in absolute darkness as far as the working of the metaphysical is concerned. He is thus unable to comprehend many events taking place in his own life and around him everyday. This evokes awe and fear of the unknown. This then leads to superstitious beliefs and irrational behaviour. What man cannot understand, he blames upon the working of some other unseen power. He terms it the supernatural.

Thus it is that different people believe in different forms of superstition depending on their own customs and traditions. While some consider the number 13 to be an ill omen, others consider the crossing of a cat in their path as a sign of bad luck. While some believe in wearing charms to keep ill luck at bay, others believe that the wearing of certain stones, rings, anklets and the like will make lady luck smile upon them. There are no rational explanations, just beliefs. The darker and more ominous side of superstition is the sacrificing of animals and sometimes even humans to propitiate the so-called "gods". Different rituals are conducted in different religions and communities as part of religious activity. Black magic, voodoo, 'spiritual' séances and such other activity like the worship of ghosts and spirits, in some of the more backward societies, are commonly associated with superstition. Any number of examples can be given of such irrational activity. There are no logical questions or answers, yet people across the social spectrum indulge themselves in such fanciful behaviour. The wonder is that even the educated do not care to distinguish between the rational and irrational. They are as much a victim of superstition and irrationality as anybody else.

Superstition will decline only when science will begin to help provide rational answers to the people. The inability of science to provide effective and alternative explanations for mysterious and unexplained phenomena certainly helps to breed superstitious and irrational behaviour. People will stop going to the quacks only if they are convinced that they can cause them more harm than good. Similarly people will stop indulging in irrational behaviour, only when the futility of such action becomes apparent to them. Will science ever be able to help? We only have to wait and hope.

Q25. It is said that the wise man learns from others' experience, the ordinary man learns from his own, and the fool learns from neither. How far do you think this is true?

A25. Experience, they say, is the best teacher. But how many people do actually learn from their own experience? Or better still, from the experience of others? Very few indeed. Does that classify the majority of the human species as fools? It would seem so from the follies that people commit again and again.

Let us first consider the plight of an ordinary person. Caught in the vortex of the world, he is tossed hither and thither in the tempest of temptation. He finds life quite burdensome and the stress of his daily work quite tiresome. He seeks a little relief in an occasional peg of whisky. In course of time he finds that the occasional peg has not only become more frequent than before, but has also grown larger in size. He knows that the urge for liquor has taken deeper roots in his mind. His better sense warns him to lay off the drink. But he is now deeply mired in the habit. Even the doctor's warning that his liver is deteriorating because of the alcohol has no impact. Till one day it is too late. The man learnt nothing from his daily experience and ultimately paid the price. He was certainly a fool.

But are we any better? Of course, not. Day after day, we read and hear about the damaging substance called nicotine in cigarettes, and how it is injurious to the human health. We nod our head in agreement and continue to smoke. We also read chilling statistics regarding the many millions who fall prey to this deadly vice year after year. We nod our head in sadness and continue to smoke. Perhaps, even more than before. We have not the courage of conviction, or the strength of character to break free from this terrible bondage. And we too pay the price. If only we had learnt from the experience of others! But alas, we didn't! And we consider ourselves wise! Fools, all!

When will the 'fool' learn to be a simple and ordinary person, learning from his own experiences? When will the simple, ordinary person graduate to the level of the wise one, who quickly learns from the experiences of others? When will men stop being fools?

Q26. The availability of easy credit helps us to enjoy the present rather than wait for an uncertain future. Discuss the extent you agree or disagree with the opinion stated above. Support your views with reasons and/or examples from your own experience, observations, or reading.

A26. The world is constantly in a flux and people are always in a hurry. The stupendous growth in science and technology has resulted in an explosive growth of new products and services in the world. The world abounds in all type of sophisticated electronic and other products, both for personal and home use, which promise to make the life of people much easier and simpler. There are of course even those products, which promote much comfort and luxury. The allure of these symbols of materialism and the desire to possess them instantly, has led to the availability of easy credit in the market place. Banks and other financial bodies are ever ready to roll out the red carpet for all those who would care to indulge in the taste of these heady comforts and exhilarating luxuries.

The people are, of course, only more than ready to buy with borrowed money. The urge to enjoy the present, rather than wait for an uncertain future is overpowering indeed. 'Why wait till one grows old and is then too old to enjoy?', seems to be the favourite dictum for the jet-age inhabitants of the exciting new world of today. Thus it is, that almost everything under the sun is acquired on credit. From expensive motor cars, sleek two wheelers, household goods, personal products and accessories, to apartment houses and cruise vacations, almost anything can be had just by flashing the plastic card or signing on the dotted line.

Although credit comes at a price, it does help one to enjoy the use of a product or service today, rather than wait till one is able to finally afford it. Not only that, one can simultaneously enjoy the use of a cross-section of products at the same time, through their judicious purchase on credit. One's existing capacity to pay could be effectively leveraged between different products, by availing suitable installment schemes offered by different companies. This would never be possible if one were to wait to buy with accumulated savings. In such a case one might be able to afford a flat, but not furniture; clothes, but not jewels; or a motorcycle but not a car. One would have the ability to buy only one thing at a time. Thus, the availability of ready credit enables one to access a diverse range of products and services without the inevitable wait.

Apart from promoting mere consumerism, the availability of credit, however, also serves bigger social purposes such as good education for the children, housing for the middle classes, and medical care in times of emergency.

While one should be careful not get ensnared into a perpetual debt trap due to reckless purchases, one can certainly benefit by prudently availing of the available credit options to buy what is absolutely essential for the present.

Q27. A prominent cement manufacturer has announced that it plans to build its latest factory in your neighbourhood. Discuss the advantages and disadvantages that will accrue to the people in your community. Support your answer with the help of reasons and/or examples.

A27. The setting up of a large factory is always advantageous to the people of that place as it helps to stir commercial and business activity in the region. From that perspective, the news of the setting up of the latest factory by a prominent cement manufacturer in our neighbourhood is welcome news indeed. However, there are also a few disadvantages that might inadvertently accrue to the local community. Let us discuss both in some depth.

First, let us consider the advantages. The setting up of the factory is sure to increase the level of business and commercial activity in our neighbourhood, because of the migration of a substantial number of employees who will be working for the company. The company is most likely to construct residential quarters for their workers. This will result in a significant opportunities of employment for the local building-construction workforce. It is also quite possible that the company may make arrangements for the setting of a school and health center in the vicinity for their employees, which will also greatly benefit the local populace. The setting up of the new factory will also see an increase in transport activity in the region, which will induce the management to improve the quality of the existing roads, and also adequately provide the neon lighting. The local vegetable market and the grocery stores are sure to do better business, as would the other shops in the area. Lastly, the increased commercial activity will be a rich source of revenue for the local council, in the form of additional taxes and duties. This will, in turn, help the council to improve the infrastructure and civic amenities in the area.

However, there are bound to be a few disadvantages, which will accrue to the local community. The increased commercialisation of the place will considerably erode the calm and tranquil atmosphere in the community. The hustle and bustle of activity arising from the manufacturing activity will be further compounded by the accentuated contiguous vehicular movement engaged in the ferrying of goods to and from the factory. The production of cement is also likely to substantially raise the pollution level in the area. The emission of smoke and other toxic material from the factory can prove to be a health hazard for the locals. It is obligatory for the M.C. to see to it that mandatory incinerators are installed to manage the industrial waste and the effluents are treated properly. The migration into the town of a large no. of outside workers may not be very conducive for the peaceful and orderly atmosphere prevailing in the area. As the additional demand for goods and services will destabilise the demand and supply ratio, the shopkeepers will have to rework their price mechanism, unwittingly hurting the local community in the process.

However, on the weighting scale, the advantages of development will tend to outweigh the disadvantages of inconvenience. Hence the move is welcome.

Q28. If you had the choice, would you prefer to live in a large city or a smaller town? Support your answer with the help of specific reasons and/or examples.

A28. I would most certainly prefer to live in a large city. A large city comes with much larger advantages than a small town. Let me enumerate the various advantages that would accrue to me if I opt to stay in a large city.

First of all, the employment opportunities in a large city are far greater than those in a small town. The presence of large business establishments, industrial houses, factories, shops, banks, restaurants and the like, ensure that there would always be a wide variety of jobs to choose from. The pay scales in a larger city would also be correspondingly higher than those prevailing in a smaller town. Also, the prospects of career enhancement would be significantly more, due to the presence of several large companies. Further, the availability of high-end jobs in various streams like finance, banking, import-export, insurance, would be confined mostly to the larger cities, since most of the bigger companies normally maintain their head offices there. It would be the same story for many government jobs, because most government administrative offices are located in the large cities.

Apart from the employment angle, a large city would offer me several other advantages, which would be missing in a smaller town. There would be no dearth of educational opportunities, due to the presence of a large number of schools, colleges, and other institutes of higher learning. Similarly, the prevalence of several hospitals and health centers would ensure that there would not be any lack of medical facilities. Also, most of the larger cities exude a metropolitan or even cosmopolitan atmosphere, which helps to improve the ambience of the place and makes life more pleasant and livable. Due to this, people are more secular minded and there are consequently less caste and social tensions. There is abundance of good drinking water in the larger cities, better housing facilities, good roads, and generally a better level of civic amenities. Public and private transport facilities are better developed, and far superior than those in a small town. There is also better road, rail and air connectivity. The presence of large shops, establishments, and supermarkets, ensure the easy availability of all kinds of products and services. The administration and governance in large cities is generally better than in the smaller towns and this ensures good law and order. ;

It is thus apparent that the general standard of living is definitely more advanced in a larger city than in a smaller town. This would invariably tilt my choice in favour of the former.

Q29. "Success in life is due to one's hard work and not luck." Do you agree or disagree? Explain with the help of suitable reasons and/or examples.

A29. It can be said that success is the fruit of hard work. Without hard work there can be no real success in any endeavour. However, hard work is not the only criterion of success. It can, at best, be said to be, one of the most important elements of a successful life, though not the only one. Luck does play a role, and a very important one, in making a man successful in his life. Let us see how.

To assume that one's success in life is entirely due to his hard work would also be to assume that man has got unfettered free will in the world. However, we know that this is not true. For instance, man has got no choice over his own birth. He can neither choose his parents, nor the time and place of his birth. His destiny is primarily shaped by the circumstances surrounding his birth. If he is born to rich parents, he automatically acquires the advantages of a good education, proper upbringing, and a healthy social life. On the other hand if he is born to poor parents, he is not so advantageously placed. These primary factors then shape his later pursuits in life like higher education, proper career, and also a good family life. These are generally extensions of his earlier years. Placed in such a positive position, the person finds it generally easy to succeed. On the other hand, a person who has been not so beneficially positioned by destiny, will find the climb to success long and labourious. Even after undergoing grueling hardships, he may find success still eluding him. It could be that due to poverty he could not acquire the type of education, which could have helped him to succeed. It could be that due to lack of resources, he could never start a business, which could have propelled him to greater success. There could be any number of reasons. On the other hand, the other person who has been better placed by destiny may succeed with comparatively lesser effort, just because luck has favoured him with better and more opportunities in life.

Again, destiny might have endowed one individual with greater intelligence than another. Thus, while the first, by dint of his superior mental capacity, may go on to become a doctor or a lawyer or an engineer, the second may have to content himself with a lesser demanding career like that of a shop clerk or a salesman. Health again, is a gift from the gods. A person who is healthy and strong is likely to succeed better than one who is ill and in poor health. Similarly, the place or country of birth plays its own role. A person born in the U.S. is sure to be more prosperous and successful than a person born in the hinterland of Africa.

It is thus obvious that success in life is determined by many factors that are beyond the control of man. If the quantum of success were to depend only upon the amount of hard work done, then the daily labourers who sweat and toil from dusk to dawn should be the most successful. But alas! It is not so. Luck does play its role in shaping the fortunes of men. Therefore, let no man boast that he alone is the architect of his life, or that his success is entirely the result of his hard work alone.

Q30. Celebrities often complain that they have no privacy because the media is always trailing and tracking them. Do you think their complaint is justified? Discuss with the help of specific reasons and/or examples.

A30. The loss of privacy is the price for name and fame. Celebrities, being public figures are bound to be under the media glare. In any case, the people who have put them on the pedestal and idolise them, have got a right to know what transpires behind the facades, and if their fantacy favourites are also real life heroes.

Celebrities should realise that they have no independent existence. They are and remain celebrities only by virtue of the adulation they enjoy among their fans. If their fans were to turn the other way, the celebrities would stand stripped of all their sheen.

Also, much of their grouse is nothing but sheer hypocrisy. After all, every celebrity revels in the media spotlight and basks in the glory of public attention. And this is all thanks to the media, which is happy to spend time and money to track their movements. It is said that celebrities can live without air, but not without the flashes of the photo bulbs. They bask in attention, and if it is missing, will actually do something dramatic to draw it to themselves. Stories are not wanting of budding celebrities bribing the members of the yellow press to publish motivated and juicy tit bits in order to catch the public eye. They feel pleased and privileged to be featured on the front covers of tabloids. Some celebrities claim that the media uses them to better their own prospects. The media claims that it is they who prospects give celebrities their status. The truth may lie somewhere in between.

44

In any case, why should celebrities object to being probed in private? What have they got to hide? If their behaviour is above board, they can very well allow themselves to be under the scanner for all twenty-four hours of the day. But are they really above board? Do they worry that if all their private escapades are splashed in public, they will no more appear as supermen and role models, but as vulnerable as clay dolls? What is it that they dread? What kind of muck do they fear that the press hounds will ferret out? Their double standards? Their fickle and questionable life style? Their social waywardness? But that may already be known. Skeletons always have a habit of tumbling out of cupboards at the most inopportune times!

Maybe they don't want their friends to know. Maybe they don't want their family and children to know. They know that fame is short-lived and public loyalties even shorter. When the glare has waned, they have nowhere to go but home.

Q31. Some people feel that it is better to save for the future, while others feel that one should spend money to enjoy the present. Which view do you support and why? Use specific reasons and/or examples to support your answer.

A31. I certainly support the first view. One should most definitely put aside some money for the future, and not fritter away everything to enjoy the present. One should always remember that the present would one day transform into the future, and when it eventually does, it should be safe and secure. Of what purpose is enjoyment today, if it becomes the cause of misery and worry in the future? It is so easy to spend, yet so difficult to save. Wisdom dictates that one must be discreet and stingy to save for the future. Let us consider why it so important to save.

The mortality rate has come down and the span of life is generally longer, but the period of earning is comparatively limited. Nobody knows how long he would live, but the age of retirement is generally fixed. One cannot work indefinitely. Therefore, during his earning span, he has to make sure that he puts aside enough money that will hold him in good stead in his later years, when he will be able to work no more. Further, the requirements in old age are sometimes more than a person's needs during the period of his youth. Deteriorating health translates into higher medical bills and hospital charges. Being weak and infirm, one needs to spend more on commuting. He will need to hire assistants to help in the house.

Next come the needs of the family. One has to provide for the education and marriage expenses of the dependent members of the family, like children and even grandchildren. One has to pay one's insurance premiums, and even for the day-to-day needs of the younger members of the family, till such time as they are employed and earning.

One may incur extra expenditure on leisure activities. People generally travel more after retirement to meet their relatives and friends who may be settled and staying far away from them.

Thus, there are so many needs that would surface in the future. Some may be quite unexpected and traumatic like accidents in the family, which may entail high expenditure. There would be the usual expenses on house maintenance and repair, and the payment of personal and property taxes.

Therefore, it is imperative that a person plan wisely for his future. If he has saved enough, he can sit back and enjoy peace and comfort in his later years and even witness the smile of joy on the faces of his children. If he has saved not, then the journey ahead would be dreary and dismal indeed.

Q32. You have just received a bonus payment from your employer. Would you prefer to buy a computer for the house or go on a vacation with your family, assuming that the amount of money is just enough for one? Give specific reasons and/or examples to support your answer.

A32. I would most certainly want to use my bonus money to buy a computer for the house. It's not that I want to deny my family the pleasure and thrill of going on a vacation, but its just that due to the paucity of the amount, I would like to correctly prioritise my spending – and I consider the computer to be a better investment.

The reasons are really not far to seek. The computer is a storehouse of rich information and a valuable knowledge base for the entire family. It will help us to better communicate with our friends and relatives, even those who are dispersed far and wide across the world. Apart from the ease of communication, it will help us save on the postage money. The children can chat with their friends from the comfort and safety of the house. It will also further the cause of their education as they can use the Internet to source valuable academic information and other material relevant to their studies. They will be able to download important data from a host of educational sites. The computer will also help me to preserve my personal files, and I could also use the financial software for the purposes of domestic budgeting and accounting. It is no doubt a valuable lifelong investment, which will pay me rich dividends in the long run.

If on the other hand, I were to use my bonus to take my family out on a vacation, we would no doubt have an enjoyable time, but it would be shortlived. A vacation cannot last forever, but a computer could – at least the knowledge that would come with it.

In fact, we could use the computer to gather information about the best tourist spots, and the special holiday packages available, which we could then use to go on a well-deserved holiday, the next time I get my bonus! Talk of killing two birds with one stone!

Q33. The past has no relevance to the present. Hence a study of historical events is of no use to us. Do you agree or disagree? Explain with the use of specific reasons and examples.

A33. I disagree with the statement. The past certainly has a relevance to the present. It cannot be otherwise. After all, the present is nothing but an extension of the past. Today is also born of yesterday. Can we then say that yesterday is of no consequence to us? There are no real boundaries in time. It is a seamless entity. What constitutes the past for us today was the present to the generation that lived then. What is the present to us today will one day become the past for a future generation. Let me explain why I think that the past is relevant to us, and therefore a study of past events invaluable.

It is said that experience is the best teacher. Man learns most by experience. Many learn from their own experiences, but the wise also learn from the experiences of others. However, our experiences are only confined to the events of our own times, whether they pertain to us or to others. When a related problem that we had faced sometimes in the past reoccurs in our life, we quickly draw a parallel with the earlier event and let the experience gained at that time act as our guide for the present. This is exactly so even with past historical events. They act as a guide and help steer us in the proper direction when faced with the present-day problems. They help us to mould our behaviour and strategies in the light of the past experiences. This is as true of countries as it is of individuals. Thus, the horrendous devastation witnessed by the dropping of the atomic bomb on Japan opened mankind's eyes to the appalling nightmare of a nuclear conflagration and led to the signing of several treaties between the leading nuclear powers for the reduction of the nuclear stockpiles in the world. More recently the events of September 11, exposed the dreadful dangers of international terrorism and helped the countries of the world to unite against this unmitigated evil. Again, a spate of hijackings in the past has forced countries to learn from their earlier lapses and strengthen their aviation security systems.

Past historical events also have a great relevance in the political and economic spheres. Many countries in the world, which had hitherto followed hard socialist and communist models, have now switched over to the capitalist and free market models, having learnt from their not so successful past experiences. In the economic domain, past historical data provides the basis of risk evaluation by insurance companies and the fixing of appropriate premiums for various products dealing with life insurance and other forms of casualty. Past data concerning various natural and geographical events is used to predict the recurrence of natural disasters like earthquakes and volcanoes. In the meteorological department, previous weather and climatic conditions are analyzed to predict the pattern of future rainfall and atmospheric conditions. This is of immense benefit to agricultural scientists. It is also of vital importance in the aviation sector, for the smooth and safe operation of civilian and other aircraft. Again a historical study of past population models is of immense help in determining the demographic trends of the future.

In the light of these revelations, it is a misnomer to say that the past has no relevance to the present, or that historical events are of no use to us.

Q34. "No risk, no gain," is the motto of some people. However others believe that "slow and steady wins the race." Which approach would you support? Give specific reasons and/or examples to support your answer.

A34. I would certainly support the latter approach. Risks are only for the reckless. A cautious and careful approach is always the safer option in life. A slow, but sustained strategy makes for safer and surer success. We have all read the story of the tortoise and the hare. Let us see more reasons why risk rarely rewards.

Risk is generally associated with greed. A greedy person is always ready to take more risk. This is best illustrated by the stock markets. People speculate recklessly by continuously buying and selling shares. Yet very few ever take any profits home. Even if they do occasionally make gains, they are invariably given back due to excessive greed. Sometimes a person's propensity for risk in the stock market lands him in dire straits. Suicides have been frequently reported by people who could not fulfill their financial obligations, having assumed unbearable and unsupportable risks. This is also the plight of several other reckless risk takers who gamble away their life savings at the casino or the race course.

People also sometimes take huge risks in their business and profession. A businessman who takes unwarranted risks and trades irresponsibly beyond his means is more likely to default in his commitments than one who is more circumspect in his dealings. A person with a more cautious bent of mind will conduct his business in a more steady and guarded manner, ensuring smoothness of his operations, which will ultimately translate into steady and sustainable profits in the long run. A good builder always builds brick by brick. Otherwise he might see his edifice collapsing before his very eyes. Again, the deeper the foundation, the bigger and stronger is the building. The structure may rise slower, but the edifice is sure to survive much longer. Several people gamble with their profession. They risk the safety of their existing job, trying to venture into greener pastures, only to find that the grass only looked greener on the other side. Their irrational, and financially risk laden vaulting from one job to another, sometimes lands them without any job on hand. Had they persevered longer, perhaps they would have risen slowly and steadily in their careers.

Then there are people who assume much risk in their personal lives. They say that they like to live with danger. Fast driving gives them a thrill. They enjoy and indulge in the most dangerous of sports and adventure. They party wildly and indulge in mindless fun and frolic. They jump from one controversy to the other. Till one fateful day they land themselves in a deep mess – sometimes unable to extricate. The prudent person goes about his tasks with care and caution, and moves ahead in life slowly and steadily. Success may be late in coming, but is more enduring.

Q35. Many government-funded schools, offering free education in some of the developing countries, are introducing a free mid-day meal scheme for the school children. They feel that this will not only encourage more poor people to send their children to school, but also improve the health of the children and increase their learning capabilities. Do you agree or disagree with this view. Give specific reasons and/or examples.

A35. This is a great humanitarian gesture and I fully endorse it, without any reservations whatsoever. Food and education for all children, particularly those belonging to the underprivileged classes of society, is their inalienable right and no society can afford to shirk its responsibility in this regard. Nothing is more shameful for any country than to have its children go without education and proper food for want of proper means.

It is in this context that the scheme to introduce a free mid-day meal for all children in the government aided publics schools in some developing countries is highly laudable indeed. In fact, this munificent scheme, which highly benefits the poor and deprived children, should be emulated and implemented by all countries of the world.

Let us enumerate the benefits of this generous gesture. It is an unfortunate, but depressing reality that in several underdeveloped and poor countries, many poor children are forced to take up work in factories and other establishments in order to supplement the very meager earnings of their parents. This deprives them of the chance of even going to a school; leave alone the other joys of childhood. Although laws have been passed in several countries discouraging this pernicious practice, the system continues to flourish unhindered due to the abject poverty of the people. If the introduction of a free meal in the schools together with free education can help wean these unfortunate children away from the prospects of child labour, and encourage the parents to enroll them in the aided schools, the scheme would have greatly achieved its purpose.

Further, the scheme also helps to ensure that at least one square meal is provided daily to the poor and deprived children. This will definitely go a long way in improving their overall health and making them physically more fit for school life. No child can study on an empty stomach. It is almost cruel to expect a child to be alert and attentive in class on an empty stomach. Thus, the provision of a proper meal during the day will not only improve the child's health, but also greatly enhance his mental ability, leading to improved performance in studies and other activities at school.

Therefore, the noon meal scheme will certainly achieve the triple objectives of improved attendance at school, better health, and heightened learning capacity, leading to better performance in studies.

Q36. Do you think that high schools should allow students to wear whatever dress they wish when they come to school, or insist on the wearing of a particular uniform? Discuss with the help of specific reasons and/or examples.

A36. Schools should definitely insist on all their students coming to school in the prescribed uniform. Let us try and understand why.

A uniform gives the student a unique identity. It reinforces in his own mind the importance of being a student and the benefits that go with it. It helps to segregate him from all others near or around him who are not students of the institution where he is studying. It gives him a better sense of belonging to his institution. It imbues him with a sense of purpose and pride.

Another very important reason why a school should insist upon a particular uniform is that it helps to bring all students on a common platform. There are then on feelings of rich and poor, or high and low amongst the students. It is a fact that various students studying in the same institution come from diverse backgrounds and segments of society. While some belong to the affluent classes, others may originate from the poorer sections of society. If each student were to be allowed to wear the dress of his or her choice, then it is very likely that while those coming from richer homes would be draped in expensive attire, those coming from poorer homes would be dressed more modestly. This may stir unnecessary feelings of envy and jealousy among some of them, leading to perhaps undesirable behaviour and awkward situations. Also if each student were to be engrossed in watching the wearing apparel of another student out of sheer curiosity or envy, or discussing it with his class-mate, it would result in unnecessary distraction in the class, apart from affecting the concentration level of the students. Another social fall-out would be that the poorer children might feel uncomfortable and perhaps even inferior as compared to their richer counterparts, and bring to bear undue pressure on their poor parents to buy better and trendy attire for them, putting the parents in great dilemma.

On the other hand, if all students were to wear the same uniform, preferably stitched from the same quality of cloth, then there would be a better sense of equality amongst them, leading to a sense of belonging and comradeship between them. This will lead to the development of better team spirit and a feeling of oneness among all the students.

They will then grow up without any sense of class or community feelings, and inferiority or superiority complex. They will share love, not animosity amongst themselves.

A uniform also does credit to the institution to which it belongs. It symbolises the principles and values that it stands for. It gives the entire institution an identity of its own. It also sets it apart from other institutions, when its students go to compete with students from other institutions on the sports field, or in inter-school debates and competitions.

Thus, the uniform lends an aura of achievement and glory both to the institution and its students.

Q37. Some people feel that advertisements by cigarette and liquor manufacturers should be banned as they encourage people to smoke and drink. Do you agree or disagree? Explain with the help of specific reasons and examples.

A37. I do agree. Advertisements from cigarette and liquor manufacturers, which extol the smoking and drinking habit, should most certainly be banned. The use of tobacco and liquor has been medically proved to be detrimental to one's health. In fact, all cigarette packets carry the statutory warning that cigarette smoking is injurious to health. Therefore there is absolutely no justification for spreading such harmful habits among the people at large through high-pitched advertising.

Year after year, one reads chilling statistics of the innumerable deaths caused all round the world as a result of tobacco consumption. A recent report stated that nearly two million people die annually from nicotine poisoning. In fact, more people die every year from tobacco-related ailments than from other natural causes. Smoking can result in various types of cancer, the commonest among them being cancer of the lungs, intestines, and all forms of oral cancer. In many countries people suffer from acute forms of oral cancer due to the habit of chewing tobacco. Countries around the world spend millions of dollars for the treatment and rehabilitation of these cancer-afflicted patients. Thus, apart from seriously impairing the health of the people, the consumption of tobacco also results in an enormous drain of governmental resources, which could have otherwise been better utilised in addressing the important basic needs of the people such as food, drinking water, health care and education.

Similarly, the excessive consumption of liquor has also been proved to be extremely harmful for the body. This insidious habit leads to a gradual deterioration in the functioning of the vital body organs such as the heart, the kidneys and the liver and often results in premature death. Apart from this, the social consequences resulting from excessive consumption of liquor are well known. Not only individuals, but also entire families have been led to complete ruin at the altar of this destructive habit. Crimes, including rapes and murders have been unwittingly committed in a moment of raging imbalance by people who lost their sense and sanity after consuming more liquor than they could safely hold. Those who recklessly consumed the liquor were themselves mercilessly consumed by it in the end.

Governments across the world have been making untiring efforts in recent times to educate the people on the dangers of the smoking and drinking habits. Several legislations have been passed banning smoking in public places. Many social organisations have also been conducting a sustained campaign to educate the people on the harmful effects of smoking and drinking. Against such a backdrop, the high decibel advertisements by the tobacco and liquor manufacturers to upheld their partisan interests are highly retrograde in nature and totally inconsistent with the laudable efforts being made by the governments and civil agencies to wean people away from these harmful habits. It has to be understood that the media being an extremely powerful medium of influence, its wrongful use for promoting the sales of cigarettes and liquor is to be discouraged.

Advertisements make the highest impact on the minds of the young, who are more prone to be easily swayed by the swashbuckling and snazzy style of campaigning. Can there be anything more disastrous for a country than to have its youthful population fall a prey to the vile habits of smoking and drinking and the resultant dangers? Cigarette and liquor manufacturers would have us believe that they are amongst the biggest contributors to the country's exchequer through the payment of duties and taxes on the sales and consumption of liquor. However the generated revenues offset the cumulative benefits as they are also the biggest source of drain on government resources as we have just mentioned earlier and a still bigger drain on the general health of a country and its citizens. The irony of smoking is that it affects not only the health of the smoker himself, but indirectly also the health of others in his vicinity who passively inhale the noxious smoke emitted by the smoker.

Public interest demands that all advertisements by the cigarette and liquor manufacturers and promoters should be legally banned.

Q38. In a world dominated by science and technology, the learning of subjects like history is becoming increasingly irrelevant. Discuss the extent to which you agree or disagree with the opinion stated above. Support your views with reasons and/or examples from your own experience, observations, or reading.

A38. Today's world is no doubt dominated by science and technology. It is a world where machines are increasingly replacing the manpower. While computers replicate the functions of the brain in the back office, robots supplement man in the assembly lines. However this does not in any way make the learning of history irrelevant. It makes it even more relevant.

History is not just a subject in school or college. It chronologically encapsulates a perfect record of past events for the benefit of posterity. The museums that we build, the monuments that we erect and the temples and churches, where we pray, are nothing but the extensions of a bygone past, which we seek to merge with the contemporary present. This gives us solace and a deep peace of mind. By visiting a museum, we are able to take a peek into the past, into civilisations long forgotten: their rise and fall. We are able to relive the majestic powers of the ancient kings and emperors, their moments of glory and their moments of downfall. We are able to wade into royal palaces and courts and get a glimpse of their majesty and their vulgarity. When we cast our eyes upon the ancient spears, the swords, the guns and the cannons we are frightened by the bloodletting they must have caused, the havoc they must have wrought in people's lives. By visiting the monument of a revered leader, we are inspired to serve, just as he must have done in his time. When we visit the ancient temple or church, we kneel down before the Lord and ask forgiveness for our follies.

History imparts us a sense of belonging and herein lies its importance. With the help of hindsight it gives us a glimpse into our past deeds. And misdeeds. Deeds and misdeeds that only history can judge. If experience is our best teacher, then there is no better guide than history. We need history today more than ever before. In place of swords, we now have lethal guns. In place of cannons we have sophisticated tanks, rockets, missiles and bombs. Our forefathers could kill only on the battlefield, but we can over-power the targets from the skies and the seas. The scope of our operations knows no bounds. After all, have we not progressed in science and technology? Someday, in the not too distant future, our own progeny will be required to judge us, and learn from our follies. And history will be their guide.

Q39. Financial gain is the only consideration in job selection. Discuss the extent you agree or disagree with the opinion stated above. Support your views with reasons and/or examples from your own experience, observations, or reading.

A39. Financial gain can be said to be one of the factors, perhaps the most important, but surely not the only consideration in a prospective employee's job selection. To analyze the issue correctly, we have to view it from two different perspectives.

First we have to look at the issue from the perspective of an absolute fresher, a student just out of college and waiting to set his foot into the world. He cannot be too concerned or particular about the salary that he would earn. His prime consideration at this stage would be to get a proper job, best suited to his qualifications and interests, and preferably with a company of repute. He would like to gain entry into an organisation, which would help in imparting the best training to him, give him hands-on exposure to important aspects of its functioning, and nurture his talent and ultimately help him to grow. His other concern would be an amiable work environment, ethical work culture and encouraging and understanding treatment at the hands of his superiors. These would be the broad concerns of a fresher in search of good employment opportunities.

Let us now look at the issue from the perspective of an experienced employee, who is comfortably perched on his office chair, yet would like to better his future prospects. This category would be more inclined to view financial gain as an important motive. He would like to move onto greener pastures, if he feels that he has already exhausted the prospects of further promotion in his existing company. Being at a middle or semiorganisation level, and having to provide for a hefty home budget, apart from savings and other investments, he would be more inclined to switch jobs for a better pay packet. Obviously, he also would like to make sure that the new work environment is equally, if not more, conducive to his tastes. Of course, if he were seriously dissatisfied with the job itself, for whatever reasons, he would not mind migrating elsewhere even for the same, if not a little lower pay.

In general, we can safely surmise that financial gain may be the prime motive in job selection, but other considerations are equally important. Women, for example, would prefer to work in a place, which is free from the usual harassment, and where there are other female employees as well. The location would be another consideration. Nobody would like to travel long and tiring distances to his place of work, if he can help it. Prospects of growth would certainly be an important concern. The larger the organisation, the better of course would be the growth prospects. As already said earlier, the work ambience and the amiability amongst the colleagues, apart from the attitude of the top management to its employees would be the other driving considerations. Convenient work timings together with adequate recreational facilities for the staff would also be other motivating factors. Perks and incentives would no doubt play their own role. And finally, the culture of work recognition and rewarding of talent in an organisation will exert their magical and magnetic pull.

Q40. Do you think that companies should reward their employees with salary hikes and promotions on the basis of their seniority and number of years of service, or purely on the basis of their performance and productivity? Explain with the help of suitable reasons and/or examples.

A40. My view is that both the set of factors are equally valid and have to be given balanced weightage for effecting salary hikes and promotions. However, to what extent the company would actually like to reward its employees would greatly depend on the interplay of all these factors and also an individual assessment of each. Let us try and understand the significance of each.

Seniority, based on the number of years of service is certainly an important consideration for rewarding an employee. This is all the more relevant today, due to the high attrition rates that companies are faced with. Many employees are quite happy to leave their current employer if they spot a little greener pasture ahead. Each new job is treated only as a stepping-stone to another better paying one. This is especially so in the flourishing Call Center and Business Process Outsourcing (BPO) businesses. Even though companies vie with one another to offer a better package of incentives to their valued employees - apart from their basic pay-in order to hold on to them for a longer period of time, they don't always succeed in retaining the loyalty of their staff. This puts an undue burden on the companies' management as also their resources, since all new recruits have again to be put through the training process. In such a scenario, an employee who has loyally stood by the company through thick and thin, and put in several years of service, certainly deserves to be rewarded with salary hikes and promotions. Further, by the very dint of his long years of service, he would have gained sufficient insight and experience of the company's line of activity, to be able to make a significant contribution towards the company's progress and prosperity in the future. It would also be in the company's own interest to retain his services through proper rewards, so that he may not be tempted to switch loyalties to some other business rival, who may offer him better pay and growth prospects in order to lure him away.

This is not to say that an employee's performance and productivity should not be an important consideration for rewarding him. In fact companies would be well advised to constantly and actively monitor the overall performance of their employees and reward them accordingly from time to time. This will increase the enthusiasm among the employees and give them motivation for optimal performance. Apart from hikes in salary, some companies, especially those operating in highly competitive businesses, also offer sales incentives and performance linked bonuses to their marketing personnel in order to induce them to give their best and help achieve the targeted figures. This is particularly true of companies operating in the financial segments like insurance, banking, and housing; travel related services; and consumer goods. Performance linked rewards not only help to better motivate the employees, but also give them a feeling of immense job satisfaction and recognition. This automatically translates into high productivity ratios for the company.

Companies should judiciously evaluate the seniority factor, the number of years of service, and the performance levels of their employees while deciding to reward them. All these factors should be considered in cohesion to arrive at a proper decision.

Q41. Do you feel that companies should recruit their employees purely on the basis of their educational qualifications and work experience or also take into count personal qualities of the candidates like work habits, broader goals and aims in life, hobbies, and other personality traits? Explain with the help of proper reasons and/or examples.

A41. Company managements should definitely take into account the individual qualities and other personality traits of candidates while considering them for employment. These should, of course, be considered in conjunction with the educational qualifications and work experience of the applicants.

Though educational qualifications and work experience are the prime indicators of a candidate's suitability for the job, the individual qualities and other personality traits would greatly determine how successful he would be in his assignment. Further, when there are several applicants with similar educational qualifications and with the required work experience, the only determining factors in the selection of the proper candidates would be the personal qualities and traits of individual candidates. Every job has its own particular requirements, and the hiring manager would have to gain a sufficient insight into the overall personality of the candidate, to determine whether he would be successful in living up to the specific demands of the job.

Educational qualifications by themselves are not conclusive indicators of the suitability of a candidate for a job. Though the quality of education received and the qualifications achieved are a general reflection of the academic capabilities and skills of the candidate, they do not by themselves guarantee that the potential employee will be able to effectively utilise his knowledge and aptly exercise his skills in real life situations while on his job. Further, the quality of education and the standard of the examinations differ from institution to institution, place to place, and country to country. In some of the underdeveloped countries graduate degrees are easily bought and sold for a price. Hence, it would be unfair to judge all the job applicants purely on the basis of their educational certificates. Also, in many countries the examination and evaluation system is based more upon the memorising of the subject matter by the student rather than a critical understanding of it. The questions are stereotyped and designed to be more a test of memory power rather than any reasoning or analytical skills. Let us now try and understand how some of the unique personal characteristics of individual candidates can reflect in the quality of their work.

One of the most important skills required in the business place is the ability to communicate well and interact efficiently with people. This calls for clarity of thought and skillfulness of communication. This quality is born of rigorous training and honed over a period of time. One who has acquired it is at a considerable advantage in dealing with a wide host of business issues, especially those requiring considerable interactive and interpersonal skills. Another desirable quality in a good employee is the ability to think critically and rationally. He should have an analytical bent of mind and the power of proper discrimination.

His hobbies would indicate how well and productively he utilises his spare time. Similarly, his aims and goals in life would provide an insight into his long-term objectives, and the roadmap charted by him to achieve his ambitions would indicate the grit and determination with which he would pursue his career. His honesty of purpose and integrity of character would clearly segregate him from the casual and the frivolous. His gentleness of manner and politeness of speech would make him an instant hit with his superiors as well as the company's customers. His burning desire to succeed would be reflected in his readiness to put up with hard work and take the most strenuous jobs in his stride.

These are some of the individual characteristics and personality traits that company managements should always be on the lookout for in prospective employees. While pure academic qualifications can only be broad indicators, these qualities alone will constitute a sure signpost for a successful career.

Q42. All countries benefit from international trade, which involves free movement of goods and services between the countries, with minimal restrictions. Do you feel that the same principle should be extended to the free movement of people between different countries for purposes of taking up employment or for doing business? Explain with the help of suitable reasons and/or examples.

A42. The two issues are very different from each other and I don't think that they can be viewed from the same prism. The first issue of international trade involves only movement of goods and services, whereas the second issue involves cross movement of people for purposes of business and employment. While the first issue, being only in the nature of a commercial transaction, resulting in the buying and selling of goods and services, is relatively simple, the second issue involves crucial factors of resident ship or even citizenship for the people migrating to the foreign country in search of employment or business, and is thus much more complex. Let us look at the matter in more depth.

International trade in commodities and services is beneficial to all the participating countries because it results in goods moving from places of plenty to places of scarcity. This helps bring about parity in pricing as well as in supplies. It helps the exporting country to profitably export its surplus production, and also correspondingly helps the importing country to overcome shortages and off-set high prices in any particular commodity in which it is deficient. Thus, it is mutually beneficial to both the trading partners. There are no other issues involved except those routinely connected with the practice of international trade and marketing.

The transmigration of people for purposes of employment and business between different countries is a different issue altogether and may not always be mutually beneficial to the countries involved. The primary concern is that the high-techies of the developing world looking for greener pastures will induce a brain-drain pattern, ultimately leading to a dangerous vacuum. It is a fact that the standard of living in some of the most developed countries of the world is extremely high as compared to that prevailing in the developing and underdeveloped countries. The earnings of the employees in these countries are also significantly high, and so are the returns on businesses, because of the higher spending power enjoyed by the people. This obviously induces people from the poorer countries to migrate to the developed nations in search of lucrative business and employment opportunities. However if this type of migration of people is to be permitted, absolutely unhindered and unrestrained, it will inevitably result in serious social and economic problems for the host country. While companies will readily hire people from the poorer countries who would be only too willing to take up employment even at a fraction of the prevailing wages, the resulting shift in the pattern of hiring will cause immense unemployment among the local people, who will then find themselves being gradually eased out of their high paying jobs. This is sure to lead to an outcry from the local populace, and eventually result in serious social problems, and perhaps even violent clashes between the locals and the immigrants. In fact this is what is being witnessed today in several parts of the developed countries, which have seen innumerable job losses on account of outsourcing of several low end jobs in the financial, technology and service sectors to the developing countries. This would also entail economic consequences, as sizeable amounts of earnings of the immigrant population would be repatriated out of the host country. This apart, unmitigated migration of people from other countries will tend to affect the demography of the local population and result in culture shocks. The recurring cases of racial disturbances, involving the locals and the foreigners, occurring in some countries are an indicator of this disturbing trend.

Another important aspect is the security issue for the host country. Unchecked and unbridled migration of people would result in several undesirable elements sneaking into the country, sometimes even through backdoor means, leading to serious law and order problems over a period of time. This could seriously endanger and jeopardise the internal security of the host country.

In conclusion, it may be surmised that though controlled migration can prove to be beneficial to the host countries as they can better access and utilise the pool of available international manpower talent – in order to complement and maximise their own knowledge and productivity in diverse fields of activity – unchecked and rampant influx of foreign workers will ultimately prove detrimental to the country's own national interests as is the case with the flux.

Q43. Do you feel that governments would be better advised to allocate more resources for the development of good roads and highways or for the improvement of public transport like buses, trains, and other modes of mass transport for the general public? Explain with the help of suitable reasons and/or examples.

A43. This is a difficult choice for the policy planners as both are two sides of the same coin, namely public infrastructure. Both complement each other and are generally ineffective and redundant without the other. It is certainly desirable to have good roads and highways, but what use would that serve if there were no proper public vehicles to ply over them? Similarly, for the efficient and smooth running of public buses and other vehicles, good roads and highways are absolutely imperative. It would seem to be the classic case of the chicken and the egg!

However, if only one alternative can be chosen due to a constraint of resources, then I would throw my weight behind increased allocation for public transport like buses, trains and other means of mass transport. This has become absolutely indispensable and has acquired utmost urgency due to the unchecked explosion of private vehicle ingress in many countries, leading to chaotic and congested traffic conditions on the city roads. This is partly due to the poor availability of proper public transport facilities, or inefficient running of the same. Many countries trying to desperately grapple with this problem are increasingly resorting to the practice of discouraging private vehicles through the imposition of heavy duties on the vehicles and collection of heavy parking fees. However, in the absence of an alternate and efficient public transport system, this would only compound the problem of the people and increase their hardships by putting additional financial burden on them. Hence the dire need for improving the public transport system.

In fact, the increase in the size of the fleet of the public buses would automatically result in additional revenues for the government, which could then be usefully deployed to improve the conditions of the roads and highways and perhaps also build newer ones. Private parties could also be roped in to build and maintain new roads and highways on toll collection basis. This would then provide an added impetus to further development of the public road transport.

Apart from road transport, governments could also allocate funds on priority basis for development of rail transport for local and long distance travel. As trains can carry a larger load of passengers, and cover longer distances in relatively shorter periods of time, an efficient rail network would go a long way in mitigating the hardships of the traveling public. Most countries have also introduced the mass rapid transport system consisting of underground tube railway in their larger and more congested cities. Another popular form of public travel consists of the sky-trains and buses, which run on elevated platforms or from specially suspended cables. As these systems of transport complement the road transport and are not hostage to the road conditions, it is definitely preferable that governments prioritise their spending in favour of such projects, rather than getting totally mired in the controversies of funds allocations vis-à-vis hard infrastructure like roads and highways and public vehicles like buses.

Q44. Describe the most important quality that you would like to see in a good friend. Support your answer with the help of suitable reasons and/or examples.

A44. "A friend in need is a friend indeed." This popular adage beautifully sums up in a few words what an ideal friend should be like.

The most important quality that I would like to see in my good friend is that of dependability in times of need. This is perhaps the only quality that sets apart a really true friend from the many fair-weather friends who always keep flitting around like garden flies on the lookout for sweet nectar from a budding flower. Such so-called friends are only to be seen when the going is good and the sun of prosperity is shining clear and bright. At the slightest sign of the gathering clouds of gloom, they quickly fade away like the short-lived rainbow in the sky. They are always in attendance when we throw lavish parties, give birthday treats, and celebrate our wedding anniversaries. They are plentiful in their praise and uninhibited in their adulation. They are ever ready to join us in the fun and frolic, generally only at our expense. They enjoy our company and hospitality at home and outside. They are never sparse in words in praise of us before others. They try hard to impress us with their loyalty by talking ill of others who they perceive to be our enemies. They often pledge that they will ever remain friends with us, and never part from us; while deep within their own hearts they know how hollow their own words are. We believe in them, and in all that they say, for who is not moved by words of praise and acclaim? Then comes the day of reckoning. There is no more partying, fun, and frolic. There are no more free lunches and dinners. There is no more the comforting bulge in our pockets. The sun has slowly set on our own prosperity. We are sad and disheartened. We are also in debt. The whiff of money has gone. And so have our "friends". They have suddenly made themselves scarce. They have suddenly discovered that they have much more important business elsewhere. This is the larger picture of life and its fair-weather friends.

The true arrive when the false depart. That is the only sign of their greatness. They were never always around when we were busy partying and impressing with our short-lived wealth. But their concern for our welfare has brought them to us even closer. They offer not just empty words of sympathy, but also a shoulder to lean on. They are like the anchor that will not let our empty boat drift. They will stick by us through thick and thin.

They will sail with us in our rocking boat, until we safely reach the shore. They alone are worthy of our love. They alone are worthy of our trust. They are not the fair weather friends. They are our dear, loving, trustworthy, all-weather friends.

Loyalty, thy name alone is friendship.

Q45. If you were a philanthropist and had the choice between funding the construction and running of a public hospital, and donating your money to a space research organisation, which would you prefer? Give appropriate reasons and/or examples to support your choice.

A45. If I were in the privileged position of a philanthropist, I would certainly prefer to fund the building and running of a public hospital. I would not want to waste my money on an uncertain and sophisticated venture like space research, which would in any case not be of any immediate benefit to the vast majority of common people.

I strongly feel that proper healthcare and medical facilities still elude a lot of poor people. It is indeed ironical that when governments are prepared to spend tens of millions of dollars to put satellites in space, or send a spacecraft to the red planet, the poorest of the poor should often be dying for want of money to buy their life saving drugs or to undergo critical surgery. A public hospital, which would offer succor and solace to the sick and treat them with care and humaneness, without extracting its pound of flesh, is in my view much more deserving of my philanthropical largesse than a space adventure.

A hospital is a living monument of care and concern for the suffering humanity. It boasts not of future conquests, as would the mighty space stations, but reaches out now and here to offer its hand of help to those who come knocking at its doors for relief from their pain and suffering. It seeks not its fulfillment in the satisfaction born of a flag planted on some distant and dreary planet, but in the look of relief and contentment on the faces of the poor suffering souls that it serves. It derives its glory not from the vain talk of space conquests, but from the looks of gratitude on the faces of its poverty-stricken poor.

When I help build a hospital, I know that my money will not go up in literal smoke in some fanciful and idealistic space fantasy, but will withstand the ravages of time and continue to serve the needy and the destitute; and the feeble and infirm. It will help to wipe a tear from the eyes of some suffering soul, and give solace and comfort to some senior citizen in the evening of his life. It will help someone to walk better with the help of an implant, and help someone to live longer with a transplant.

Long after I am no more, the hospital will still be there to serve continually. The players would have changed, but the play would still be the same. A new generation of patients and a new generation of doctors – but human suffering as it always was.

Q46. Some countries ban the airing of many international programs and channels on their television for fear of adversely affecting their society and culture. Discuss the extent to which you think this is true or justified. Support your answer with the help of appropriate reasons and/or examples.

A46. Countries that ban the airing of many international channels and programs in their territories do not always do so out of any bona fide fears or concerns regarding their national interest. Many a time the ban is imposed selectively to block those channels, which are perceived by the ruling politicians in the country, to be inimical to their political interests. The ban is generally imposed in those countries that are ruled by dictatorial and autocratic elements, which fear that constant exposure to the international media might awaken the people of their country to their basic fundamental and democratic rights and stir pro-democracy and freedom movements on their soil. The media in their own country is generally tightly gagged and allowed to broadcast only such material that is favourable to the ruling clique.

Some countries, especially those founded on religious lines, are ruled by fanatic religious leaders or groups. In such places theocracy prevails and the country is generally governed with an iron fist by the theocratics. Democracy is almost totally absent, and religious laws, howsoever outdated and obsolete, are strictly implemented and ruthlessly enforced. Punishments for violations are often very severe and sometimes arbitrarily imposed. Death by stoning and beheading for very serious crimes like murders, rapes and drug peddling, and amputations of the limbs for crimes of a slightly lesser nature are not uncommon. Women's rights are almost non-existent and the genders are generally segregated in public places. Women have to adhere to the dress code – a head to toe covering is strictly enforced in public places.

Entertainment, as is normally understood in any free society is not allowed. Movies and local television programs, including news broadcasts, are closely monitored to adhere to the official state policy. Dissent of whatever nature is not encouraged and any form of agitation for human rights or a democratic way of life is often put down with brute force. The justification trotted out is invariably always the same – anti-religious conduct will not be tolerated.

Is it any wonder then that international channels and programs that reflect the values of democracy, freedom and human rights are always banned in such places? Men and women are looked upon and treated as different animals. Male superiority and domination in such societies is almost complete.

The state media is often used to indoctrinate the people according to the ideals and beliefs of the ruling class. The people have no choice except to toe the state policy.

Leaders in such countries fear that the sobering and awakening influences of the international media might be detrimental to their vice-like grip on their subjects, and thus take every step to insulate their people from its influences.

Q47. "All people glorify and enthusiastically talk about human virtues and morality, yet very few people actually live up to them." Do you agree with this statement? Explain with the help of appropriate reasons and/or examples.

A47. Human nature is very frail. It is true that all people extol and glorify human virtues and eulogise the benefits of morality, yet very few indeed live up to the lofty principles, which they themselves so often enunciate.

Why is this so? Partly, because of the hypocrisy deeply ingrained in the human mind. We always expect the most exacting standards from others, but never from ourselves. We are quick to criticise others and point out their faults, but never ever look to our own. Rather, we feel that we do not have any. Thus, we fly into a rage whenever anyone points out our own faults to us or even mildly criticises or rebukes us. We believe that we alone are the paragons of all virtue, while all others are only sinful souls. We have oft heard that, "To err is human, to forgive is divine", yet we naively believe that we are too great and wise to ever err. Only lesser mortals around us do the erring. We are quick to criticise, forgetting that "to forgive is divine." We justify our censure of others by saying that it is in their own best interest. Yet we never apply the same yardstick to ourselves when others criticise us.

Many a time, we take the high moral ground and mouth virtues just to impress others. We like to build a façade of 'holier than thou' halo around us. We like to portray ourselves before the world as role models of virtue and morality. Of course, we have something to gain. We always do. It could be that there is some monetary gain to be had. It could be that our smooth talk would land us a plum job. It could also be that we want to project ourselves as messengers of virtue before our friends, relatives and society in general. People are generally impressed by high decibel clichés and we hope to win their respect and admiration by our grand exposition of the virtues.

Sometimes our glib talk of morality is just to camouflage our own weaknesses. We subconsciously know all our failings and frailties, and also know that we have not the requisite mental strength to mend our ways. We do make feeble attempts sometimes to overcome our weaknesses, but generally the mind proves much more stronger than our own conscience. When we begin to fall in our own esteem, we try to convince ourselves that we are really not as bad as we think we are. Do we also not talk of virtues and morality? If we were absolute sinners, would we ever have such thoughts cross our minds? We try and soothe our embattled soul with empty words of virtue.

We all talk of virtues; yet practice them in a way that suits us best. We loudly proclaim that honesty is always the best policy, yet we find nothing wrong in cheating the State of its tax dues. We agree that to be truthful is the best policy, yet at our own shop we have no compunction about selling outdated goods to our customers, telling them that they are absolutely new. We moan in agony when our car inadvertently runs over a cat, yet we daily partake of the flesh of slain animals to please our palate. We counter vegetarianism by asserting that god meant animals to be our food, while all the time we keep proclaiming that all living beings are creatures of the same Father. We aver that it is not good to be greedy, yet our own avarice knows no bounds. We tell others that it is not good to be covetous, yet we ourselves keep burning in the fires of envy and jealousy. We say it is good to be kind, yet we never stop piercing other hearts with our unkind words. We say that we should always be generous and forgiving, yet we never stop to criticise.

Will man ever learn to walk the talk?

Q48. Doctors state that more and more people are beginning to suffer from stress related illnesses nowadays, due to the pulls and pressures of modern day life. Discuss to what extent you agree or disagree with this opinion. Explain with the help of proper reasons and/or examples.

A48. It is true that stress related illnesses are on the rise. More and more patients frequent their doctors seeking relief from stress related disorders. While some display only milder indications of stress like headaches, body aches, loss of sleep, giddiness and nausea, and the like, others exhibit much more serious symptoms like high blood pressure, palpitations, heart problems and diabetes. If left unchecked the initial symptoms could ultimately mature into full-blown diseases and disorders.

What could be the reasons for this new-age malady? Why is stress playing such havoc in people's lives? Let us probe deeper.

Stress could either be due to psychological or physical causes. Defined as any interference that disturbs a person's health, mental and physical well being, stress generally occurs due to angst and when the body is required to perform beyond its normal range of capabilities. The term stress is often used to denote tension or anxiety.

There is no doubt that the hectic pace of modern life is the prime contributor to human stress. People's expectations and values have undergone a sea change over a period of time. Overweening ambitions, ever-growing desires and a tendency to become more and more materialistic has become the order of the day. We all want to be rich and successful and for that we struggle very hard and that takes a toll on our health and consequently increases stress. In the highly competitive world of today, the word "failure" has become a taboo. We set targets that are sometimes wholly unrealistic and then work beyond our endurance to try and achieve them. When we are unable to do so, we become extremely frustrated and stressful. Our desire to lead highly materialistic lives and our passionate yearning to enjoy all the material comforts of the modern age are the prime culprits that often land us in stressful situations. This blind urge to over-indulge ourselves makes us live beyond our means and often leaves us with a load of borrowings. When we later find that we are unable to extricate ourselves from this vicious cycle of debt, we become extremely nervous and stressed.

Stress is also sometimes due to extremely high level of expectations from an overly demanding society. The burning desire to excel in every field of activity sometimes becomes counter-productive. Thus, we have the phenomenon of children sometimes suffering from nervous breakdowns before or during the examinations, and even seasoned athletes developing stress induced cramps on the sports field.

The changing values in society have also contributed in no small measure to stress-related problems among the people. People have generally become more individualistic and self-centered. Constant bickering and intolerance amongst married couples are leading to a rising number of divorces. Growing levels of discord and dissension in the household are seeing frequent breakup of many family units. These social factors invariably and inevitably lead to extreme builtup of stress amongst the family members, particularly the young and impressionable children. Further, the increasing tendency amongst some particularly the youth to live a life of passion and indulgence, sometimes totally divorced from ethics and morality, is also a strong contributory factor to social strains and consequently individual stress.

Stress can sometimes also result from situational factors over which an individual has no control, such as an accident or death in the family, illness, altercation with a neighbour, unexpected financial loss, and the like. It can also be the result of one's peculiar personality traits and characteristics, and lack of coping skills. One with a consistently negative bent of mind is likely to encounter more frequent and greater stress levels than others.

In the final analysis it would indeed seem that the complexities of modern living have generated greater levels of stress in society in general and individuals in particular. If people were to seriously imbibe the age-old virtues such as simplicity, love, and contentment, and shun the evils of greed, jealousy, avarice, vice and immorality, mankind might have finally found a lasting cure to the malady called stress.

Q49. Some countries have abolished the death penalty, while other countries are still retaining it. Which do you think is the better option? Explain with the help of specific reasons and/or examples.

A49. This issue has consistently aroused strong emotions among people on both sides of the divide and has been vociferously debated in almost all the important forums around the world. Still, there is no unanimity of views even among the legal and constitutional fraternity, or the governments of the world. Every time a death penalty is imposed in any prominent case, which has caught the media glare, a fresh round of debate is unleashed and there is considerable outpouring of public sentiment on both sides. The arguments are generally the same and repetitive in nature. However they do serve to constantly focus attention on an issue, which has consistently agitated the minds of even the most stoic thinkers.

To come to a rational conclusion whether the death penalty is indeed warranted and should countries do away with it altogether or not, we must first understand and critically analyze the oft-repeated arguments for and against the death penalty.

Let us first start with the arguments advanced by the protagonists of the death penalty. The most common argument in favour of the death penalty is that it serves as a strong deterrent against heinous and horrendous crime. Next, it is asserted that awarding death penalty to a convicted murderer or rapist is the logical culmination of the law of natural justice. After all, has he also not mercilessly snuffed out the life of some other living human, or brutalised the modesty of some innocent woman? Is not the victim of his appalling crime entitled to equivalent and like justice? It is also argued that such hardened and depraved individuals would pose a constant menace to civilised co-existence, and by awarding them death, society would be purged of their evil presence. The proponents of the death penalty also urge that it is naïve to assert that even the worst criminal deserves to live and should be given the chance to reform.

Let us now consider the arguments advanced by the expostulators of the death penalty. The general and wide-ranging question often posed by this school of thought is: Is there any place for capital punishment in a modern and civilised society at all? The argument generally built around this line of thought is that life is God given, hence no man has the right to extinguish it; not even the legally constituted State. Mahatma Gandhi summed up this moral view in the following words: "I cannot in all conscience agree to anyone being sent to the gallows. God alone can take life because he alone gives it."

The abolitionists assert that the modern state is meant to rise above an eye-for-an-eye approach of pre-democratic societies. It is supposed to maintain civility and decency in society through a judicial system that punishes without exception those who commit crime, but resists the temptation of playing God. By delivering the death sentence, the state, which is a temporal entity, impinges on the inviolable right to life of an individual. They emphasise that the idea of retributive justice, which is actually a medieval concept, can have no place at all in a civilised society. They also question the premise that the death penalty is an effective deterrent against crime. There is no conclusive empirical basis to the claim that the death penalty puts off or discourages potential criminals. They emphasise that the most effective deterrent is, in fact, the certainty of punishment rather than its severity. The death penalty augments state authority, compromising democratic institutions without restoring order in the process. The death sentence is also indefensible because it rules out individual reform.

Human rights groups have also strongly argued that awarding death to a person is an irrevocable act. Once done, it cannot be undone. What if the convicted person is later proved to have been actually innocent? In fact the last person to have been executed in the UK, was years later found to be innocent. This would indeed be a travesty of truth and justice. Also, in highly sensitive or emotive cases, there is no guarantee that justice will not miscarry in the face of social pressures for conviction or the presence of an overzealous prosecution. Moreover, a further problem with the application of the death penalty is that it involves a great deal of judicial discretion; as a result, whether a person is hanged or not depends considerably on the views of a particular judge. The possibility of judicial error in a penalty that is (uniquely) irrevocable is one of the truly frightening features of capital punishment.

A careful reading of the arguments advanced by both the votaries and the disapprovers of the death penalty show that both have their merits and demerits. While it is true that the prevalence and award of the death penalty has not altogether prevented the recurrence of heinous crime, it is equally true that the repeal of this extreme penalty may in fact embolden many more criminals to resort to murderous and violent crime.

Also, if we were to question the concept of retributive justice, then we would be questioning the very concept of punishment per se. A depraved killer or a homicidal rapist cannot claim immunity from death or his inviolable right to life, if he himself has not respected another human's right to life and dignity. He cannot claim humanity from a community, which he himself has chosen to traumatise and brutalise. He must realise that he does not have any rights outside the community. It is only by virtue of being a member of such community that he or she can legitimately claim any human rights privileges or legal safeguards. But these assurances come at a price, which minimally includes the obligation to honour and respect the life of other members of the group. All heinous crimes, by their very nature, destroy this compunction compact in the most violent manner possible.

As to the fears that an innocent person may be inadvertently hanged, through a miscarriage of justice, it needs to be emphasised that, that alone cannot be the sole reason for abolishing the death penalty. It would amount to throwing out the baby with the bathwater. Rather every country should put in place sufficient legal and constitutional safeguards to ensure that there is not even an infinitesimal chance of an innocent man being sent to the gallows. All death sentences imposed by the lower courts should be mandatory reviewed and reaffirmed by the respective benches of the higher courts, including the Supreme Court, and presided over by no less than 5 judges. It generally happens that even after the highest court has upheld the sentence, the convicted person files a mercy petition before the President of the country. It is only after the disposal of this final appeal that the sentence is carried out, and that too if the petition has been rejected by the highest constitutional authority in the country. Also, it needs to be mandated that the death sentence should be handed out in the "rarest of the rare cases", as has been explicitly laid down by the Supreme Court in India. Only the most appalling and horrifying crimes falling in the exclusive domain of the truly despicable and the shockingly heinous cases should attract the death penalty and a deterrence for the flagitious.

In conclusion it need to be emphasised that the death penalty need not be viewed as an "eye for an eye" form of retributive punishment, but as the ultimate assertion of society's highest form of disgust for humanity's worst depredations and a deterrance for the flagitious.

OO

"Analysis of an Argument" TASK

Introduction

In this section, the candidate is required to critique a given argument by discussing how well reasoned he finds it. Whereas in **"Analysis of an Issue"** task, the candidate can formulate and **present his own perspective** on the topic, substantiating it with the help of suitable reasons and examples, in **"Analysis of an Argument"**, his task is to consider **the logical soundness of the given argument,** rather than agree or disagree with the position it portrays.

The task generally consists of a small passage where a group of events is interpreted in a particular way, or some line of action is recommended by the writer, based on his reasoning and evidence. The candidate is expected to understand, critically analyze, and evaluate the logical soundness of the writer's claim, and present a written critique on it. It is important to remember that the candidate is not required to judge whether the statements in the argument are true and authentic. Rather, his job is to evaluate and discuss whether the conclusions and inferences drawn, based on the statements in the argument are justified and valid. He is not required to pass his opinion on the stated claim – whether it is true or false. Instead he is expected to critically analyze the thought process and reasoning that underlies the stated position and elucidate on it. He is not called upon to express his opinion on the stated position per se, but on the soundness of the logic on which the argument is sustained. In short, what is sought to be tested by this task is the critical thinking abilities of the candidate, and his analytical skills in presenting a well-reasoned written critique of the argument.

The prime purpose of this exercise is to judge the candidate's ability to effectively and insightfully analyze an argument or claim formulated by another person, and present a well structured written critique of it.

Hints on Writing the Response

These are again explained in great detail in the official GRE Program guide and readers are strongly urged to refer to the same for an in-depth understanding of the response strategies. However a brief outline of the broad approach to be followed in planning and presenting a proper response has been given here to help readers understand how to go about their task.

The candidate should first carefully read the passage, if necessary, more than once, and clearly understand the thrust of the argument. He should carefully note what is explicitly stated or claimed. He should also understand what is not explicitly stated, but implied in the stand. He must also make a note of what is offered by way of proof or evidence in support of the claim. He should also be able to understand which assumptions made in the argument are not justified or backed up by viable evidence. He must look at the common thread of logic running through the argument and evaluate if it is sound. It is also important to look at the general thrust and structure of the argument and the way in which different elements are sought to be linked together to form a particular line of reasoning. He should determine whether such elements are comparable or compatible with one another or not.

Having completed this preliminary assessment, the candidate should now proceed to sit in judgment on the underlying rationale and logic in the argument. He should decide if any competing events or alternate explanations could have caused the events in question, apart from those stated in the claim. If there is a strong possibility of other equally effective alternative explanations for the events in question, then the original argument becomes less tenable, since the other alternate causes could also be the movers behind the stated events.

The argument will generally cite specific examples to support its reasoning. The candidate should try and think of as many counterexamples as he can to dent the supporting evidence.

He should also consider what other evidence could possibly weaken the argument.

Conversely, he could also consider what other evidence or reasoning could have been adduced to further reinforce the claim.

Having broken down the argument into its individual components and having discovered the weak links in the chain, and the glaring fallacies inherent in the statement, the candidate should now use his writing skills to present a well-reasoned, well-structured, well-formulated and forceful critique of the claim.

He can organise and develop the overall response in any manner, which will most effectively communicate his analysis of the claim. He is free to question the centrality of the argument by questioning the basic assumption or set of assumptions on which the argument is founded, or the very logic reasoning on which the claim is structured. He can question the analogy drawn between dissimilar and disparate elements, which have been interwoven in the argument to arrive at a particular line of conclusion. He can also question the relevance of the stated factors, which have led to a particular interpretation of the given events, or the fallacy or inconsistency inherent in the interpretation itself. What ultimately matters is the depth and insightfulness with which the argument has been analyzed and the clarity and cogency with which it has been effectively articulated before its intended audience.

Model Arguments and Responses

Chapter II contains **43 Model Argument tasks** and their Responses. Care has been taken to make the selection as wide and diverse as possible so as to make it representative of a host of varied themes. It is again emphasised that there are no "set" or "correct" answers to any task. It is not so much the structure or configuration of the response that is important as the analytical aspect on which it is founded. Each response will differ from the other depending upon the perspective and insightfulness of every writer. No two responses can be exact, either in content or in style. The purpose of the Model tasks and the sample responses in this Chapter is to give some broad idea to the candidates as to how to proceed in breaking down or analysing the arguments into their various individual components and spotting the fallacies in the claim, explicit or implied. It is also intended to familiarise the readers with some basic writing skills and presentation strategies. It has however been clarified that the Test examiners will not be looking for any particular writing strategies learned in English composition or college courses. Nor will they be looking for any particular mode of writing or developmental strategy. Candidates are free to structure and organise their response in whichever way they feel will be best suited to effectively articulate their views. What is important is the level of critical thinking and analytical reasoning that is inherent in a response.

Note: Readers may also refer to the subject matter under the heading "Model Issues and Responses" in Chapter I for further details and comments, which have not been included here in order to avoid needless repetition.

OO

Model Responses

Q1. Following appeared as an advertisement in the newspaper from the tobacco industry:

"Of late, the government has taken several harsh measures to curtail the use of tobacco by the people. These include imposing unbearably high duties and taxes, ban on cigarette ads in the media, and banning of smoking in public places. The government claims that this is done with a view to prevent cancer-related deaths. Yet the fact remains that not all cancer is caused by smoking, and not every smoker dies of cancer. On the other hand the industry contributes millions of dollars in taxes to the exchequer every year, which can be used by the government to build schools and hospitals for the people."

Discuss how well reasoned is this argument.

A1. The argument put forward by the tobacco industry in justification of the use of tobacco by the people is specious indeed. No doubt it is intended to be self-serving and hence it can be considered to be motivated. The argument needs to be put in perspective so that the readers are not fooled by the charitable camouflage that it dons.

The argument loudly proclaims that not all cancer is caused by smoking. This may be true, but it does not detract from the fact that smoking is also one of the important causes of cancer. In fact the incidence of mouth, throat and lung cancer is attributed predominantly to the prevalence of the smoking and nicotine constituted tobacco chewing amongst the habituals. It is also an admitted fact that smoking-related cancer accounts for the highest number of cancer-related deaths in the world. The fact that cancer can also be due to other causes, cannot justify in the least that nicotine-induced cancer should be viewed with a benign eye. Can a judge acquit a man accused of causing death by rash and negligent driving, on the grounds that death on the roads is also caused by so many other factors? A devious argument indeed!

As if adding salt to injury, the argument goes on to claim that not every smoker dies of cancer. Small mercies indeed! The fact that "not every smoker dies of cancer" in no way disproves that many smokers in fact do die of this scourge every year.

As if to camouflage its sins and atone for its wrongs, the industry proudly proclaims that it contributes millions of dollars every year to the exchequer, which could be used to build schools and hospitals for the people. It is to be noted that taxes paid constitute only a small portion of the total profits that the industry makes, the rest being retained as its own wealth. In any case, the mere fact that the industry pays huge taxes cannot be justification enough for the havoc it wreaks on the hapless smokers. Surely no amount of money earned by the exchequer can compensate for the life of even one person who dies in the process. The benevolent suggestion that money earned from the taxes paid could very well go to build schools and hospitals is also an insult to the memory of those who die every year at the altar of this multi-billion empire. The moot question is whether one social evil can be traded off for one social good. Even otherwise, the loss on account of the government spending every year on the hospitalisation and other expenses of those afflicted with the deadly cancer, together with the loss in general productivity on account of these premature deaths in society may far outweigh what it earns by way of taxes from the cigarette industry, making it appear a pittance in comparison.

From all accounts it is more than obvious that the argument is logically untenable and morally bankrupt.

Q2. At an economic seminar held recently, one of the speakers had this suggestion to offer:

"The best way of overcoming our huge balance of trade deficit is by levying further duties on the biggest item of import, namely, oil. Oil results for more than 40% of our imports. Evidence suggests that when the last such hike was effected, the domestic consumption of petroleum products came down by nearly 10%. As the trade deficit is still alarmingly high, it makes eminent sense to further hike the duties substantially. In this way we can steadily reduce the deficit.

Discuss how well reasoned is this argument.

A2. The above argument is clearly based on the data provided which reveals that the consumption of petroleum products in the domestic market came down by 10%, subsequent to the effecting of the hike in oil duties earlier. There are two aspects to this argument. One pertains to the reliability of the data itself and its proper interpretation. The other pertains to the ultimate result based on the action taken on the lines stated in the argument. Let us examine both.

First, in the absence of evidence to the contrary we will have to proceed on the assumption that the data regarding the decline in the petroleum consumption, subsequent to the first hike in the duties is correct. That done, we will have to see if the data has been correctly and logically interpreted. The argument has assumed that the reduction in consumption is directly related to the hike in the duties of imported oil. Is this really so? After all, there could be several other factors that could have negatively impacted the consumption in the petroleum products. Let us try and enumerate these factors.

First, the reduction in consumption could be purely for economic reasons of demand and supply. It is quite possible that due to recessionary conditions that might have been prevailing at that point of time, the demand for petroleum products from the industry might have come down sharply. Similarly there might have been lowered demand from the road transport sector. As recession impacts travel and tourism, it is also quite possible that there might have been a significant decline in the consumption of aviation fuel used by airliners. In this way, lowered demand from several sectors of the economy could have added up to an average reduction in consumption patterns by about 10%. It is also possible that the hike might have been effected during vacation period, when the density of population is much lower, people having already left on holidays. This will automatically bring about a reduction in the consumption from the transport and household sector. The decline could also be attributed to the enhanced electrification of cooking systems in the home and a shift from diesel run locomotives for the railway to those run on electricity. Finally, the decline in the domestic consumption of oil products could also be due to seasonal factors. For example, in winter, there is additional demand for fuel due to heating requirements. This is not so in the summer months.

When so many alternative factors could have produced the same result, it would be hazardous to rely on the data provided without additional substantiation from other sources. This gives rise to the possibility that the data might have been misread. In fact the best way to substantiate the argument would be to show that the oil imports have actually declined after the hike in duties was effected. However there is absolutely no data in the argument to suggest this. There is also no data available to suggest that the hike in duties has in fact improved the balance of trade deficit.

This then takes us to the second stage of the argument. What would be the consequences if the data has actually been misinterpreted as suggested above? In such a scenario, if the decision to effect a substantial second hike in the duties on the petroleum products is actually implemented as stated in the argument, the consequences could be disastrous. Petroleum products being the most essential items of consumption, the people and the industries will have no choice except to buy them at the new prices, notwithstanding the hike in duties. This will most likely lead to a cascading inflation in the

74

economy in general, negatively impacting the living and saving standards of the population. An undesirable fall-out of this phenomenon would be a likely weakening of the country's currency in relation to the other free currencies of the world. This will in turn make further imports of oil even more expensive, leading to a vicious circle of price increases. Further, the costlier inputs, including oil itself, will make the country's exports uncompetitive and unviable, leading to an even greater aggravation in the trade deficit. This cycle could prove disastrous for the country.

The obvious conclusion is that any decision based on the obvious misreading of the sketchy data provided in the argument is most likely to have deleterious consequences for the country.

Q3. A trade paper carried the following observation in one of its editions:

"The price of fruits has gone up steeply over the last several years. For example, while apples were being sold at 30 cents a pound at 'Super Mall' about 9 years ago they are now being sold there at rate of over 2 dollars a pound. The weather having remained largely stable over this period, the obvious conclusion would be that the apple growers are to blame for the exorbitant rates prevailing today. This calls for strict price controls in the interest of the consuming public, and suitable measures should be taken to ensure that the growers do not continue to raise prices in this manner.

Discuss how well reasoned you find this argument.

A3. The argument is totally flawed because it most thoughtlessly assumes that the rise in the price of apples sold in 'Super Mall' from 30 cents a pound about nine years ago to over 2 dollars a pound at present is solely due to the overpricing indulged in by the growers of the fruit. This is rather a naïve and simplistic assumption as it is based only on consideration of a single factor, while totally ignoring the rest. Let us consider the facts in closer detail and identify the various other factors that could have influenced the rise in the price of the fruit either individually or in combination.

Firstly, the stated rise in price from 40 cents a pound of apples to over 2 dollars at present has taken place over an extended period of nine years. Is it rational to assume that the price of any commodity would remain absolutely static for over a decade in the face of ever rising inflation and cost of living? In a scenario of growth and prosperity, the prices of various commodities tend to rise due to excessive demand. Secondly, assuming that the fruit is grown locally, it is quite probable that excessive export of the fruit due to strong overseas demand has correspondingly reduced supply in the domestic market, leading to a firming up of the prices. Conversely, if the fruit is being imported, an excess of domestic demand in the exporting country or other overseas markets may have impacted supplies, and consequently, prices in this country. Thirdly, the rise in prices may also be due to an increase in profit margins on the fruit by Super Mall due to higher overheads involved or other business considerations. It may be due to better quality of the fruit sold at present or even due to superior packaging. It could also be due to a rise in freight and other costs involved in transportation of the fruit from the production centers to the retail outlets.

Fourthly, even assuming that the apple growers are charging a higher price for the fruit now as compared to about a decade ago, it is quite fair to assume that the cost of various inputs such as seeds, fertilizers, pesticides, and other factors of production like ploughing equipment, tractors, power supply, and even land would have risen in tandem with the general levels of inflation, thereby forcing the growers to suitably revise upwards the price of their produce. It is also possible that the tax rates and other government levies on the farm produce could have been raised upwards, resulting in higher prices at the production centers. It is also possible that due to un-remunerative prices prevailing earlier, many growers of apples might have switched over to cultivation of other varieties of fruit or vegetable, thereby resulting in inadequate supply in the market place and consequently enhanced price.

Therefore it is absolutely absurd and unfair to blame just the growers of the fruit when a slew of other relevant factors enumerated above could also be in operation. Most importantly, it should not be forgotten that the cultivation of fruit by farmers who are widely dispersed geographically, is a highly competitive activity and not monopolistic in nature. The prices are determined by the forces of demand and supply and not arbitrarily or in isolation, as if there existed only one group of growers. Thus, the argument propounded is not only illogical in nature but also in contradiction to the laws of economics.

In the light of the above facts, the suggestion at the end of the passage that strict price regulations are called for to prevent the growers from further raising the price of the fruit is not only economically absurd and legally impracticable, but if at all implemented would have just the opposite of the intended reaction, as farmers would then be forced to curtail production of the fruit due to unviable and un-remunerative prices, leading to a real scarcity situation with abnormal rise in prices.

Q4. The Morning Herald was the highest selling daily newspaper in the State a couple of years ago, but it now seems to have fallen on bad days. Ever since the introduction of the Evening Star, the daily evening newspaper, about a year and a half ago, its circulation has declined steeply. The management feels that the best way forward would be to reduce the price of the newspaper to make it more competitive vis-à-vis the Evening Star. Not only will this increase circulation by bringing back the earlier readers who might have shifted loyalties to the new paper, but also result in more advertisement revenues due to the increased readership.

Discuss how well reasoned is the argument.

A4. The management of The Morning Herald obviously feels that it can win back its earlier readers who might have shifted their loyalties to the Evening Star simply by reducing its price to make it more competitive in comparison with that of the latter. This conclusion has been reached on the sole assumption that price is the only motivating factor which influences the readership of a newspaper. This assumption is rather shallow and simplistic. While embracing this line of thought, the management of The Morning Herald has overlooked several other factors that might have played an important role in the people of the State opting for the Evening Star. Let us try and analyze what other factors may have motivated this change in the people's preference.

The first and most glaring fact relates to the time of delivery of the two newspapers. While The Morning Herald is obviously delivered at the start of day, the other is supplied in the evening. This factor alone could make a huge difference to several readers of the newspaper, especially those who leave early for work and thus do not find time to read the paper in the morning when it is delivered. This class of readers would ideally read the paper in the evening after returning from work. It is for this class of people that the Evening Star would make eminent sense, as it would cover the current day's events apart from the earlier news. Why should they buy The Morning Herald in the morning only to come back and read it in the evening, when they could catch up with the latest events of the day by buying the Evening Star? This would equally apply to the student population.

The second reason could actually relate to the news content. It is quite possible that the articles of news and editorial reviews of the Evening Star are more informative and enlightening. Their layout may be superior and the graphics pleasing to the eye. The paper quality may also be better. It is equally possible that they pack much more content in their newspaper than their rival publication. They may be adding a free supplement with their regular paper containing additional coverage on sports, entertainment, shopping and other city highlights. This would automatically put them in the premium slot, and win them new readers.

It is also possible that the Evening Star apart from its other strengths may have an aggressive sales and distribution network which helps in the smoother and quicker delivery of the paper to its readers.

When any or all of the above factors may be working against The Morning Herald, rather naive on the part of its management to believe that they could win back their circulation just be reducing their price. After all, all newspapers are priced most competitively and a little reduction in the price will hardly impact the readers. They are more likely to be drawn by content than by price. Hence it is obvious that the business decision of The Morning Herald is not sound as it is based on an incorrect assumption. It would be better advised to conduct a more detailed market survey in order to establish the reasons for the loss of its readership, before it takes corrective steps. Lowering the price when it is already faced with the prospect of diminished sales may in fact seriously affect its cash flows adversely.

Q5. The following appeared as a comment in a daily newspaper:

The increasing rate of crimes in the country can be directly attributed to the disastrous impact of scenes depicting violence and sexual abuse in movies. As this adversely impacts the values in society, government should take steps to ruthlessly censor or even ban such movies. In any case persons below the age of 18 should not be allowed to view such films. Suitable legislation should be enacted for this purpose.

Discuss how well reasoned is this argument.

A5. Crimes in society are as old as society itself. To attribute crime in a country just to the portrayal of violence and sex abuse in movies is nothing but an exercise in self-delusion. After all movies are a fairly new phenomenon. Can it be stated with conviction that there were absolutely no crimes before the advent of the silver screen? No, Sir! Thus the reasoning that crime is the outcome of violence and abuse being shown in movies is totally illogical and carries no conviction.

The underlying assumption in this claim is that everyone who watches violence and sex abuse in a movie is so negatively impacted as to indulge in such acts in real life later. However is that really so? If that were true every person in the audience would commit one crime or the other even before he were to reach home after the show! As almost everybody watch movies, then based on the assumption in the argument, every adult, should have turned into a criminal by now! This is simply ridiculous.

The argument would also seem to imply that people who come to watch movies have absolutely no wisdom of their own and would be so overawed by what they see on the screen that they would themselves turn into criminals. It would also imply that the people in the audience have no emotional maturity or any sense of right and wrong. It also implies that they are an immature lot with absolutely no control over their faculties. No statistics have been advanced to prove that movies have such an effect on people as to result in increased crime rates in a country. In fact the opposite may be just as true. Arguably almost every movie concludes with the message that crime does not pay. The

78

villain who indulges in mindless violence or sexual abuse is almost inevitably bloodied either through his own misdeeds or through the strong arm of the law. This should, if anything, have a sobering effect on the psyche of the viewers even if a few amongst them are actually prone to violent behaviour.

The suggestion that such movies should be banned or ruthlessly censored also reveals illogical reasoning. Movies intrinsically are no more than a healthy means of entertainment for the people at large. In fact it can be forcefully argued that by showing violence and abuse in their raw form, movies just might succeed in creating a feeling of revulsion in the minds of the viewers for these despicable acts and thereby exert a sobering effect on society in general.

The other suggestion that persons under the age group of 18 should not be allowed to view such movies and that a suitable legislation should be enacted for such purpose is also redundant, as it is not based upon sound reasoning. The obvious assumption that a person less than 18 years is likely to be more impressionable than a person older than him lacks credibility, as it is not supported by any credible proof. If such were the case then only juveniles would commit all crime. However police and prison records would show that criminals belong to almost all age-groups. It can also be argued that most people tend to exhaust their innermost fantasies through their screen characters. If movies depicting violence and abuse were banned, there would then be no mental outlet for these subconscious emotions.

It may be worthwhile to consider what alternative factors could result in the prevalence or increase of crime in a country. Crime can almost always be linked to socio-economic factors afflicting an individual or a group of individuals or a country in general. High levels of poverty, squalour and unemployment in a country provide fertile ground for crime and abuse. Other reasons could be war, civil commotion, revolution or insurgency. Crime, especially against women, could also be the result of domestic disharmony, or the result of a very repressive or male-dominated society. It could also emanate from racist and communal tendencies in some countries. It could also be the result of extremely poor governance and an ineffective judicial system.

Thus, almost any number of reasons could be attributed to the increase in crime rates in society and therefore to single out movies as the main contributor to this menace is illogical and based on wrong assumptions. The contention therefore lacks conviction.

Q6. A survey conducted at one of the leading airports in the country to gauge passenger services came up with the following report:

"Fifteen out of the one thousand passengers interviewed reported that baggage handling procedures were very poor and needed to be improved. Twenty

79

passengers complained that the toilets were in poor condition, while 9 passengers stated that there were not enough telephone booths within the airport area."

Based on this the airport authorities concluded that as the number of passengers who had complaints in each area of operation amounted to no more than 1% to 2%, there was absolutely no cause for concern as the overwhelming number of passengers who constituted 98% were quite happy. Hence there was no need to allocate extra funds to improve amenities at the airport.

Discuss how well reasoned you find this argument.

A6. The argument is myopic in vision as it fails to read the larger picture in spite of the adverse comments of a fair number of passengers who were interviewed.

Concluding that the overwhelming 98% of the passengers are happy, on the premise that no more than 2% of them have complaints to make is like missing the trees for the woods. The argument fails to take into account that a survey is generally representative in nature and indicative of the larger trend.

It is important to note that only a small sample of 1000 passengers were interviewed out of several lacs who would in all probability be frequenting the airport, which is supposed to be a leading one in the country.

Let us split the argument into its basic elements and analyze each separately. First, according to the survey report 15 passengers out of 100 complained about baggage handling procedures. This would constitute 1.5% of the interviewees, who might have faced some serious problems. It is quite likely that many more passengers, who pass through the airport everyday, may have some minor problems as well in the baggage handling section, but who tend to take these in their stride as a traveling hazard! If ignored, these minor problems might one day become major in nature.

Second, 20 of those interviewed reported that the toilets were in poor condition and needed to be improved. Here, unlike as in the baggage handling, the view of the passengers, even though they constitute no more than 2% of the interviewees should be taken to be representative of the whole. The veracity of this aspect of the complaint can easily be established by doing a physical check of the toilets during the busy hours. It is quite possible that the toilet section is understaffed or ill equipped, hence the complaints from the passengers.

Third, about 1% of the passengers interviewed stated that telephone booths were in short supply within the airport area. In an age of technological innovation, when practically every passenger who travels by air is likely to be the owner of a mobile phone and consequently the usage of an airport booth would be a lower priority, it is quite serious that even then a shortage of telephone booths is being felt. Obviously the number of complainants would get magnified several times over, but for the availability of cellular phones. Hence the figure of 1% is not fully representative of the actual truth.

Apart from these obvious errors in assessment, it should be noted that the survey reveals that a total of 44 people have some grievance or the other against the services provided at the airport. Taken in its totality, this figure accounts for 4.4% of the total interviewees. It can also be presumed that the actual figure could be still higher, since many of those interviewed may not have had the time or inclination to dwell deeper on the issues, perhaps for lack of time. Some might have been even too modest to complain. Hence, it can be inferred that everything is not fit and fine in the realm of the services provided at the airport, and certainly strong corrective steps need to be taken to rectify the situation and address passenger grievances.

In conclusion it can be stated that this instance provides a classic example of a complete misreading of the available data, either deliberately or otherwise.

Q7. As e-mail is quicker and virtually free, more people are relying on this type of communication for both business and social purposes. This is likely to seriously affect the revenues of post offices, as fewer postage stamps will be sold. To compensate for this loss, post offices will be better advised to raise the prices of the postage stamps and all other services offered by them. This will help to generate additional revenues, which can be used to offer more amenities to the public visiting the post offices.

Discuss how well reasoned is this stance.

A7. While it is true that e-mail is quicker and virtually free, it is also equally true that not everyone or every place has access to it. The above stance presumes that e-mail will almost entirely replace physical mail and hence seriously impinge on the postal revenues. This is a debatable point and needs to be better analyzed. It must not be forgotten that personal and business use of computers is a relatively new phenomenon and confined mostly to the urban populace. Computers are expensive, and so are the costs that accompany them in the form of connectivity and other charges. Hence not everybody can be the owner of a computer. The computer density is still quite low in rural areas. Further, e-mail, though offered as a free service by some leading providers, does entail charges in the form of connectivity as already stated and which is generally dependent on the time of usage. This would also be true of those who use the cyber-cafes. Further, for an e-mail to be effected, both the parties involved must have access to a computer or a neighbourhood cyber-café. This may not always be true. As far as rural areas are concerned, the people living there may have absolutely no access to Internet for want of proper communication infrastructure, and hence would rely solely on the local post office to receive and deliver their mail. Further, e-mail is mostly confined to informal communication of a personal kind. Formal letters, including business and legal documents, bulky correspondence and parcels have still got to be delivered via the physical mode through the channel of post offices. Also, the explosion of economic and business activity in recent times means that additional business letters, brochures and bulky company reports have to be carried by the postal department. This means that there will always be a place for postal services, irrespective of technological innovations in communication systems, of which electronic mail is foremost. Hence the base assumption that this will seriously affect the revenues of the postal department seems to be unfounded and illogical. Neither has any data been advanced to substantiate this fear. The entire premise seems to be based more on conjectures and guess work.

If the basic assumption has been shown to be flawed, the ostensible remedy suggested is even worse. An increase in the rates of postage stamps is sure to hit only the poor who do not have access to computers and have no choice except to continue to use the postal facilities. This would then constitute a serious disservice to the vast masses of the ordinary people, who the post office as a public utility is committed to serve at the most nominal rates. Others may be forced to look for better alternatives, like courier services for delivery of parcels and letters and banks for transfer of funds. Hence the step is likely to prove counter productive in the long run, benefiting neither the post office nor the people at large.

As the conclusions reached are based on incorrect assumptions, the post office would do well to reconsider its decision to raise prices.

Q8. A year-long study conducted by the traffic police threw up the following report:

Ever since the mobile phones were introduced in the market, there has been a gradual increase in the general accident graph involving motorists. Many of those involved in accidents were found to be speaking on their instruments while driving. This proves that the usage of mobile phone while driving is the main reason for the increase in driving accidents and should thus be banned by legislative action.

Discuss how well reasoned is this argument.

A8. This argument is built up on three basic issues. Firstly, that there has been a progressive rise in the general accident rate involving motorists. Secondly, this is surmised to be from the time of the introduction of the mobile phones in the market. Thirdly, many of those involved in the accidents were found to be conversing on the mobile phone while driving. A brief analysis of each of these issues is necessary to establish the veracity of each.

The first issue pertains to the rising accident graph over a period of time. This by itself is of no special significance. It is a fact that accidents do rise over a period of time, with the rise in the population levels, as well as the density of the vehicles on the road. Accidents also rise due to poor infrastructure like bad roads, congested roads and street lighting; poor traffic sense amongst the drivers and a lack of road safety consciousness among the pedestrians. Unmanned cross-ways and the absence of four-way broad lanes is another trigger-off. Poor policing and law enforcement are the other contributors. Hence this issue in no way substantiates the main argument.

Let us now turn to the next issue. It is claimed that the accident rates have been on the rise ever since the introduction of the mobile phones. This also does not conclusively prove that the rise in the accident levels is solely on account of the use of mobile phones while driving. At best it may be purely coincidental, and at worst may only be one of the several contributing factors in an accident. We should not lose sight of so many other factors that may be the direct cause of accidents on the roads. Let us enumerate a few. Several traffic studies have proved that many accidents are caused by the carelessness exhibited by the pedestrians who tend to dart across the roads unexpectedly and fail to use pedestrian crossings and under-bridges and over-bridges. They are also caused by bad roads, poor lighting, and sometimes by impaired visibility due to fog or snow. Over-speeding amongst a section of the drivers, rash and negligent driving and overloading of the vehicles are some of the other causes of serious accidents. In the presence of so many alternate causes, how can it be conclusively surmised that the only cause of accidents is the innocuous looking mobile phone?

Let us now analyze the third and final issue in the argument. It has been stated that in many cases the drivers of the motor vehicles involved in the accidents were found to be conversing on their mobile phones. This again may be purely incidental. For the argument to be absolutely clinching, the stated cause of the accident – in this case the mobile phone – should always be proved to be the immediate and proximate cause of the accident. Here it is not so. It is also possible that drunken driving is one of the causes of the accident, even though it may not be the only one. It is equally possible that some of those who were driving and conversing on the mobile phone, were also driving in an inebriated condition, and the accident had more to do with their disoriented mental condition than with the conversation per se. Any amount of theorising is possible, but nothing conclusively proves that the rise in the accident graph over a period is the direct result of conversing on the mobile while driving.

This is not to say that conversing on the phone while driving does not distract the attention of the driver and could not result in an accident. It certainly could and therefore this dangerous practice should in effect be discouraged, if necessary by legislation. But to eliminate all other possibilities pertaining to the cause of the rising graph of accidents is to close one's eyes to reality, which may in fact be counterproductive and detrimental to the introduction of counter measures to reduce the incidence of road accidents.

Q9. The following is an excerpt from an article that appeared in a business journal:

High rates of taxation encourage people to adopt unfair means to evade taxes, leading to fall in government revenue. Hence tax rates should be suitably slashed to encourage more people to comply with taxes. This alone will result in a broadening of the tax base and generate additional revenues for development.

Discuss how well reasoned is this argument.

A9. For a rational analysis of this argument we will have to consider some of the complex issues involved in taxation together with a basic understanding of human psychology and behavioural patterns.

The incidence of high taxation is directly linked to the fiscal needs of a particular country, its developmental plans, and the prevailing economic situation in general. Though high taxes do constitute a heavy burden on the taxpayers, yet, the pressing need to garner substantial resources by the government sometimes make them inevitable.

The thrust of this argument is that if taxes are high, the tendency to evade is equally high, and conversely if the taxes are low, there is a readiness on the part of the people to comply fully and honestly. This, it is claimed will not only result in a widening of the taxpayers base, but will actually result in higher realisations.

How far is this true? Let us examine the matter more closely.

When we assume that a lowering of the taxes will automatically induce honesty in tax payment and consequently result in more people coming forward to pay their taxes honestly, we are presuming that the tax collections are dependent solely on the goodwill of the people without much of administrative compulsion or pressure from the government. In reality this is not so. People pay high or low taxes not out of choice but out of compulsion. Who would like to pay taxes if he had a choice? Thus, if tax rates were to be lowered without corresponding action and initiative by the government to stringently enforce the lower tax regime and actually bring more people in the tax net, the results could prove disastrous for the state exchequer. Thus, this argument would survive only subject to the caveat that the lower tax regime is actually accompanied by stringent tax collection measures on the part of the government.

Secondly, a mere arbitrary reduction in tax rates across the board may not be the only panacea for garnering higher resources for development. It has to be understood that the widening of the tax base implies that the cost of tax collection and administration will also rise manifold. As this new base of first time taxpayers are likely to be on the lower fringe of the tax bracket, it has to be ensured that the cost of collection does not fully or substantially eat away the additional revenues garnered. This then would be the second condition, the fulfillment of which together with the first condition mentioned earlier could alone ensure the survival of the argument. In the absence of these conditions precedent, the argument would automatically collapse.

Q10. The following is an excerpt of a speech made by the candidate of the National Labour Party in the run up to the State Election:

"The National Democratic Party has now been in power for the last 5 years. This period has witnessed chaotic conditions in our economy. Inflation is at its worst. The cost of housing and food has gone up steeply, making the life of the poor miserable. Privatisation of government companies has led to retrenchment of several workers due to closure of loss making divisions of such companies by the company managements. Fixed annual bonuses have been replaced by performance-based incentives, which are not favourable to the workers. The price of petrol and diesel has been raised several times. If our party is voted to power, we shall revoke all these economic excesses and ensure labour friendly policies. We shall ensure that the price of oil remains stable, notwithstanding external fluctuations. All these measures will help growth as the economic condition of the people will be more stable."

Discuss how well reasoned this argument is.

A10. The political strategy outlined by the National Labour Party is as hollow as the argument advanced by them. The argument seems to be structured and orchestrated more with an eye on winning the election, than for doing any real economic good to the people of the State. Let us now consider how the electorate should view this argument.

Firstly, their view that the previous dispensation has indulged in "economic excesses", which they promise to "revoke", needs to be closely examined. According to their own statement, the state is witness to high rates of inflation. Inflation is an economic phenomenon and the government of the day cannot be held solely responsible for it. Inflation could be due to any number of factors, both internal and external, over which the ruling party may have little or no control. In such a situation, it is only natural that

85

there will be an all round increase in the price of all commodities, including food, and housing.

Secondly, they have criticised the retrenchment of labour and replacement of annual bonuses with performance-based incentives. Both the arguments lack credibility. In an inflationary environment, which entails spiraling costs, is it reasonable for any private management to hold on tenaciously to a loss making division and continue to pay wages to its labour force? If so, how long would the company survive? Further, performance-linked incentives, rather than fixed bonuses would ensure greater productivity for the company, and thereby higher rewards for the workers.

Thirdly, their grouse that the prices of petrol and diesel have been raised several times also does not cut much ice. It is well known that most countries almost fully import their requirements of oil, hence external fluctuations in the prices of crude, will necessarily require suitable proportional adjustment in the local prices of oil. To assume otherwise would be to wish bankruptcy for the local oil companies. And this is exactly what the National Labour Party have promised; that they will not raise the price of oil, notwithstanding external fluctuations.

Let us now analyze the manifesto of the Party if voted to power. They visualise growth, by "revoking" the "economic excesses" of the ruling party, adopting labour friendly policies and by keeping the price of oil "stable", even in the face of external fluctuations. They feel that this will bring more economic stability in the lives of the people and thus promote growth. Their entire line of reasoning is seriously flawed, deliberately or otherwise, as subsidisation of oil, irrespective of the external fluctuations, will only plunge the oil companies into bankruptcy. The bulk of 70 per cent export of oil entails thousands of crores of fiscal burden on the government-kitty and the prospect of oil subsidisation is simply not viable. This will not only throw the entire fiscal situation of the State into serious disarray, but also negatively impact all other industrial activity, fuel is basic ingredient in the cycle of mobility. Ultimately, this will fuel inflation further, and perhaps result in great turmoil and unemployment in the state. Therefore, this model of "growth" is not sustainable and in the long run will seriously jeopardise the very interests of the labour, which the National Labour Party, so zealously seeks to promote. Thus the electorate would do well to properly assess the arguments forwarded by them, as they seem very unconvincing.

Q11. The Sales Manager of a prominent general store dealing in groceries and provisions called "Super Store" outlined the following business strategy to its board of directors: "The Store's sales have increased by more than 25% this year since the addition of a pharmacy section and coffee bar serving light snacks. This proves that customers will opt to purchase from a one-stop shop. Hence the board of directors should sanction the required funds for adding other departments dealing with wearing apparel, furniture, jewellery, and computers. This is sure to increase sales figures substantially and result in higher profits."

Discuss how well reasoned you find this argument.

A11. The business strategy outlined by the sales manager of Super Store is seriously flawed because it is based on erroneous assumptions and inadequate data of the total sales, or its complete misinterpretation. The business manager has assumed that the increase in the total sales of the store by 25% is entirely due to the addition of the pharmacy section and the coffee bar. In the absence of specific sales figures of each of these divisions, it is futile to jump to hasty conclusions regarding the contribution of the new division to the total sales figures. For a proper analysis one needs to know the total amount of stock holding and cash investment of each section and the corresponding sales figures of each. In the absence of such data no credible conclusion can be reached. It is quite possible that the major chunk of increase in sales has actually come from the main business of the store, namely, groceries and provisions, while the contribution of the newly added sections may be negligible in comparison. In fact the increase in sales may be due to a variety of factors unrelated to the addition of the new divisions, such as better business conditions in the current year, increased advertising or partly due to actual increase in the merchandise cost due to inflationary pressures.

Even assuming that the pharmacy division and coffee bar have in fact contributed in some measure to the enhanced sales, it needs to be analyzed if the actual profits generated there justify the additional investment and operating costs incurred on these. Otherwise the shop space thus utilised could perhaps have been more prudently used to add newer products related to the store's existing line of business.

Be that as it may, the manager's request to the board of directors to sanction extra funds to add further new divisions such as wearing apparel, furniture, jewellery, and computers is absolutely alarming. After all, the store's existing line of business is arguably confined only to items of daily use like groceries and provisions, which have a ready market in the form of households and hotels. Pharmaceutical products can also be classified in the category of essentials, as they constitute a medical necessity. A coffee bar serving coffee and light snacks can also be termed more as an auxiliary service to the customers to enhance their patronage to the shop. However, the move to add the four new departments as enunciated by the sales manager assuming that they will lead to increased profitability for the store is fraught with danger. The underlying assumption by the sales manager seems to be that every department will result in increased sales and hence increased profitability for the store. Both the assumptions are questionable. All the four new departments envisaged by the sales manager are unrelated to one another and totally unconnected to the core business of the store, namely, groceries and provisions. It is foolhardy to assume that a housewife shopping for groceries will end up buying expensive pieces of jewellery, or a patient coming to purchase medicines will opt to place orders for furniture or computers.

It is also more likely that those who wish to purchase wearing apparel, jewellery, furniture or computers will want to visit specific shops and showrooms dealing in these items for better variety and fixed prices. Such items are unlikely to be purchased from a store whose main line of business is confined to groceries and provisions.

Thus, an ill-conceived entry into unrelated and obviously capital and cost intensive business as those planned by the sales manager may end up totally ruining the store's financial stability. It is also to be noted that higher sales figures per se do not automatically result in higher profitability. It is entirely possible that the increased sales may not be sufficient to justify the burden of additional investment and costs and may in fact prove detrimental to the overall profitability of the business. In such an eventuality the losses incurred on account of the new divisions may in fact totally wipe out the profits generated by the store's core business of groceries and provisions, and perhaps even plunge the business into huge and insurmountable losses.

It can thus be concluded that as the very assumptions of the sales manager are seriously flawed, no credible business growth strategies can be based on them.

Q12. In a report by the marketing division of a leading manufacturer of fluorescent tube lights it was stated: 'The sales figures of ordinary brand of tube lights have taken a hit ever since the company launched a premium deluxe brand of tube lights which is priced nearly 40% more than the former, but lasts for twice as long. The newer brand of tube lights were launched about a year ago and accounts for this year indicate that the profitability has also declined substantially. Obviously this is due to lower repeat sales on account of the longer life span of the new deluxe brand. Hence to increase profitability, we should discontinue the manufacture and sale of the new brand and revert to the manufacture and sale only of the ordinary brand.

Discuss how well reasoned this argument is.

A12. This is a classic case of a clash of interests between the marketing and manufacturing divisions of a company. The manufacturing division has introduced a superior product with the ostensible purpose of enhancing the sales and profitability of the business, while the marketing division feels that this very step has been detrimental to its overall profitability. An ironic situation indeed!

Let us consider the merits in the arguments put forward by the marketing division and see if they are valid. Firstly, for lack of sufficient data, it cannot be presumed that the dip in profitability is entirely due to the fall in the replacement market due to the longer life span of the new product. After all, if the tube light lasts longer, it also costs 40% higher. This difference in price may not be entirely due to the additional manufacturing costs, but also additional profit margin due to the launch of a superior product. If so, then it should actually add to the overall profitability of the business or at least compensate for the perceived fall in the replacement market. Secondly, the fall in the sales figures of the earlier product are most likely to be offset to a great extent by the sales of the newer one. Thirdly, the fall in profits may be due to totally unconnected issues like a hike in the cost of raw materials, additional taxes and duties, higher fixed operating costs such as employee salaries, rents, power bills and the like. The fall in sales of the earlier brand may also be due to the changing preferences of the customers. who would now wish to purchase superior products in the market. It is also possible that the company's competitors have already introduced a similar product of superior life span in the market. In such a scenario the company has absolutely no alternative except to come out with a matching product. Failure to do so might seriously impact the general image of the company in the market place and render its product line obsolete and redundant. In such circumstances, the company will suffer grievously if a product which has been rendered obsolete either due to changing preferences of the consumers or by the competitive market forces is not immediately replaced by another more acceptable one of superior qualities.

In fact, the introduction of a technologically superior product always bodes well for the future growth and profitability of a company. Killing a superior product in favour of an inferior one due to a fallacious interpretation of the profitability factor is sure to recoil devastatingly on the company in the long run. Reverting to an obsolete product is a retrograde step and might even wind up the company.

Further, in the absence of relevant data of the exact replacement time cycle of the earlier product, the profitability results based on just one year since the introduction of the new product, may not reflect the actual picture of the replacement sales.

Also, the pessimistic premise put forward by the marketing division does not take into account the fact that the introduction of the new deluxe brand of tube lights may in fact enhance the overall sales figures of the product since it will bring in its wake newer customers resulting in a gradual shift to the company of a substantial slice of the business of its competitors. This will in fact result in a multiplier impact, as a higher base of an original product sales will ultimately bring in a correspondingly higher replacement market corresponding to the life span of the new product.

Thus, the recommendations of the marketing division are based on mistaken assumptions and incorrect reading of the profitability trends and as such the argument lacks any conviction.

Q13. The following was a remark made by the Finance Manager of a Business Process Outsourcing company:

Three years ago we were paying $ 1500.00 per month to our middle-level employees. Today we are paying $2000.00, which is almost 33% more than our earlier scales. During this period the profitability of the company has declined by nearly 10% though sales have risen by nearly 30%. Obviously the increase in the salaries has proved counterproductive. We should therefore revert to the earlier pay scales. The money thus saved could be used to explore new business opportunities. Discuss how well reasoned is this argument.

A13. The Finance Manager of the Business Process Outsourcing Company has based his reasoning on certain business assumptions. The first obvious assumption is that the profitability of the company has come down by 10% in spite of the increased sales due to the additional burden of the higher salaries. The next assumption seems to be that the employees whose salaries had been raised have done nothing to earn the extra money being paid to them. The third assumption is that the employees will continue to work for the company even if their salaries were reduced to the earlier levels.

Let us now analyze how rational are the assumptions of the Finance Manager. In the very first instance, he has erred in assuming that the profitability of the company has come down just because of the additional burden of the enhanced salaries. The very fact that the sales have shown a nearly 30% jump in the relevant period shows that the employees have actually done their best and helped to boost the company's sales. If in spite of this the net profit of the company has declined by about 10% during this period, it could be due to any number of reasons. It is possible that due to increased competition for available business in the market, the company has had to substantially reduce its profit margins. It is also possible that fixed and other variable expenses of the business might have gone up during this period and due to the reduced profitability the business has not been fully able to absorb them. It is also possible that the business may have suffered some losses on account of bad debts and these have been reflected in the reduced profitability.

It may also be that high long-term expenses capitalised earlier have been written off during this period. The reasons could be many, and none of them may have any bearing upon the staff salaries.

The second assumption of the Finance Manager that the employees have done nothing to earn the extra money paid to them is factually incorrect based on a reading of the sales figures, which show a healthy 30% growth in sales. In fact, it would not be wrong to infer that had it not been for the enhancement in the salaries paid to the middle-level employees, the sales might have actually remained stagnant, for lack of proper motivation amongst the staff.

The third assumption on the part of the Finance Manager that the employees would remain loyal to the company and continue to serve there, in spite of a reduction in their salaries is no more than wishful thinking. After all the salaries have risen by 33% over a period of three years, which translates into an increase of just 11% per year. This is quite normal in any business. Perhaps the company has been forced to increase the salaries of its employees in line with the prevailing levels offered by its competitors. In such a situation, if the company goes ahead and reduces the level of salaries, the employees may be left with no option except to look for other jobs in the market. This will surely prove detrimental to the interests of the company, as it will lose its experienced staff to its rivals, which might then result in business migration to its competitors.

In such a situation, the Finance Manager's dream that the money saved can be used to explore newer business opportunities may turn out to be only a fond hope, for want of proper employees.

The reasoning of the business manager is totally flawed as it is based upon incorrect assumptions and a misinterpretation of the available data. The argument thus lacks credibility.

Q14. The Secretary of a local youth association submitted the following petition to the Licensing Department of the Traffic Police:

A school survey has shown that more and more parents prefer that their wards to use their cars to go to school, rather than use motorcycles in view of the rising accident rates involving two-wheelers. As such, the government should seriously consider reducing the age limit for issue of driving licenses from 18 at present to 15. After all, if there is no age bar on the old for driving motor vehicles, why should there be on the young? In fact the young are more healthy, alert, agile, and enjoy better eyesight and hearing.

Discuss how well reasoned you find this argument.

A14. This argument is built up on only one main parameter, and that is the health angle.

It is openly questioned that while there is no bar on the older people driving motor cars, why should there be any restriction on 15 year olds from obtaining motor licenses.

It is stated that the younger people in fact enjoy better health, are more alert, agile and enjoy better eyesight and hearing.

The argument is weak and unconvincing because it does not take into account the fact that physical health alone is not the criterion that determines the age at which one can obtain a driving license.

In determining that a person can apply for a driving license only at the age of 18, it is implicitly recognised that one should have stepped into adulthood before he can be permitted to join the driving fraternity on the roads. Obviously, what is considered important is not only the health of the individual, but also the general mental and emotional maturity of an elementary kind. After all, driving on the roads is a very serious business, since at stake are the lives and limbs of innumerable road users, including pedestrians. The moot question is whether a 15 year old has the mental makeup and maturity to understand the serious responsibility cast upon him while driving on the roads. Any misdemeanour on his part can not only prove fatal to him, but also cost someone else his life or limb. In his youthful exuberance, which is common at his age, the 15 year old may want to indulge his favourite racing fantasies on the crowded city roads, or pamper his petty ego by reckless overspeeding and overtaking of other vehicles. He may care little for the safety of the little children, the old and infirm, and other pedestrians as he drives wildly across pedestrian crossings. He may think it fashionable to jump signals and disobey other road rules. In the process, he may wreak havoc on himself and others. The point is that he is too young to understand the trauma involved in a road accident or the suffering of the victims. The older person on the other hand, having observed life from closer quarters, would be much more careful and circumspect.

The argument is flawed even if viewed from the legal angle. If a 15 year old can claim the rights of an adult of 18, then he should also be ready to subscribe to the responsibilities that come with them. After all, an adult can be convicted of manslaughter and even jailed if it is conclusively proved that he has caused death of another by deliberate rash and negligent driving. The 15 year old on the other hand, being a minor, is not likely to be dealt with in similar fashion.

In conclusion, it may be stated that ordinary driving does not demand any exceptional hearing, eyesight, alertness or agility. Normal functioning of these faculties is sufficient. Hence the comparison drawn with the older people on this count is not valid. The argument is thus weak, unconvincing and devoid of any substance.

Q15. The following is a memo circulated by the marketing group of ADB Constructions:

Newtown is the fastest developing industrial town on the coast. Many new industries have been set up and new roads and bridges are being built. Consequently the population of the place has increased by more than 25% and with growing employment, family incomes have risen much quicker and higher than the country average. Surveys across the country reveal that the average demand for bigger homes costing $1,00,000 and above far exceeds that of budget homes costing lesser. Therefore in order to maximise our profits, we should plan to build only the high cost houses in Newtown to take advantage of the faster economic development that is taking place here.

Discuss how well reasoned is this argument.

A15. The argument suffers from several infirmities and mistaken notions. Let us analyze the matter in depth.

The decision to build only high cost homes in the range of $ 100,000 and above is based solely on the readings of a survey which found that the average demand across the country for high cost homes in that range far exceeded that of budget homes costing lesser. What appears to have been overlooked is that this is a national survey, and the results represent only a national average. It does not in any case reflect specific local trends, which may vary from place to place depending upon the local factors prevalent. As far as Newtown is concerned, the data suggests that this is a fast developing and upcoming industrial town, which has also shown the highest development, compared to other places on the coast. The fact that new industries have come up and new bridges and roads are being constructed indicates that the town is now in a stage of welcome transition. It is also stated that the population has increased by 25% and due to enhanced employment opportunities and fast-paced development, the family incomes have risen faster and higher than the national average. On the basis of this, it is inferred that there would be more demand for high cost homes than low cost budget houses, more so in the light of the revelations of the national survey on housing demands. Is this a rational conclusion? It does not appear to be so. Let us consider why.

Firstly, as the data suggests, Newtown is an industrial town, though a fast growing one. By the very nature of things, an industrial town is likely to be inhabited more by the working classes than the city elite. The boom in industrial development in a place is inevitably followed by a substantial migration of workforce from neighbouring and far-flung areas to that place. This obviously accounts for the increase in the population by nearly 25%. This surely throws up substantial demand for housing, but of what kind? The rise in family incomes in Newtown have been stated to be the fastest and highest compared to the national average, but it should be remembered that these are not in absolute terms but only on a percentage basis. Let us elucidate with an example. Let us presume that the average national family incomes have risen by 10%, while those for Newtown have risen by 15%. Based on this, a family with business, professional, or other income of $2500 per month would now be earning $ 2750 per month, whereas a family of presumably industrial workers in Newtown earning approximately $1000 per month would now be earning $ 1150. In real terms, this would mean that while the former is earning an additional $ 250 per month on a higher base, the latter is earning a lower amount of $150 on a lower earnings base.

The critical question is: Can a family of predominantly industrial workers with a lower earnings base afford high cost houses in the range of $ 100,000 and above? The obvious answer is a firm no. In such a scenario the authenticity of the argument based on the data provided immediately falls flat. It is obvious that a misreading of the available data has led to wrong assumptions, leading to faulty decision-making. This is not to suggest that high priced housing of the type contemplated by the builders will have absolutely no market in Newtown. Far from it. Industrial development of a place will also bring in its wake the entrepreneur and managerial classes, but they alone cannot project the whole market for the type of product being envisaged. If the houses to be built are to have an open market they have to be primarily targeted at the increasing ratio of the working classes, and this calls for construction of low cost budget houses, albeit proportionally.

Q16. According to the brochure brought out by the Department of Tourism, the number of people traveling to New City has risen substantially. This is borne out by the fact that the arrivals recorded at the domestic airport in the last twelve months totaled nearly 200,000 against the previous year figures of 150,000. Similar trends have been noticed from the records of the railway station and local bus station. Obviously, tourism to New City has received a big boost from the Museum of Contemporary Art and Architecture and the new Aquarium that were opened to the public last year. Thus, efforts should be made to open more such Museums and Aquariums in other cities as well.

Discuss how well reasoned you find this argument.

A16. The Department of Tourism has assumed on the basis of the increased arrival of people to the airport, railway station, and local bus station, in the current year, that tourism has received a big boost, and this it is felt, is presumably on account of the Museum of Contemporary Art and Architecture and the new Aquarium that were thrown open to the public last year. Both the assumptions seem to be misplaced, if the available data is viewed in the proper perspective.

Firstly, the argument is primarily based on the increased arrival of people to the City. It is stated that 200,000 people arrived at the domestic airport this year, against the previous year's figures of 150,000. This implies an addition of nearly 33% over the figures of the previous year. Similar trends have been observed at the railway station and the local bus station. However, this does not imply that all the additional people who arrived are tourists per se. It is also possible that they are business travelers, foreign students, diplomats or others on a personal visit. It is also quite possible that due to some additional facility introduced at New City in the past year, the city is being used as a transit point. Further, no data has been provided regarding the arrival of people during the earlier years. It is possible that the arrival of people a year ago had come down drastically from earlier period for unknown reasons, and the extra arrivals in the present year are only a continuation of the earlier patterns. If such were actually the case, then the data provided for the present year would be of no particular significance.

Another reason for the higher arrivals this year could be due to some extraordinary event being organised in New City in the current year or due to enhanced employment or business prospects.

It is also very difficult to visualise that people would come by planeloads and trainloads just to visit a newly opened Museum or Aquarium in the city. After all, would the money spent by an ordinary tourist on expensive travel and tour and lodging and boarding arrangements justify the visit to a city just to see a Museum and Aquarium, howsoever compelling they may be?

The argument is obviously flawed in the sense that it has relied on incorrect interpretation of the available data, which in itself is quite scanty. The argument would have carried more conviction had it been based on the number of people actually visiting the Museum and the Aquarium. This taken in relation with the total arrivals in the city would have given a truer picture.

Q17. A recent survey found that while middle-aged customers spent an average of nearly 35% of their money allocated for retail shopping by purchasing their requirements at department stores, younger people surprisingly spent only 20% in similar fashion. As demographic studies show that the number of middle-aged people will increase significantly over the next decade or two, it can be presumed that department stores will do substantially better than ordinary stores. To further capitalise on these trends, department stores in future should increase the product lines related to the middle-aged consumers, while simultaneously reducing those for the younger consumers.

Discuss how well reasoned you find this argument.

A17. While the argument has rightly considered the demographic changes in society, it has erred in incorrectly evaluating the available data. Let us consider how.

It has been stated that middle-aged customers spend 35% of the money allocated by them for retail shopping by purchasing products at department stores, against the lower figure of only 20% spent by the young in similar fashion. Based on this data, it has been hastily concluded that department stores will do very well in the coming years, in the light of the current demographic trends in society indicating a significant growth in the middle-aged population over the next decade or two. Impelled by this line of reasoning, it has in fact recommended that department stores increase the product lines for the middle aged customers in future, while at the same time reducing those related to the younger customers.

Let us consider in detail each aspect of this argument. In the very first instance, the argument has committed a blunder in interpreting the respective percentage figures. In the absence of absolute figures, plain percentages can be sometimes quite misleading. The pro-rata absolute configuration only can set the tone of the current trend base. It is fairly reasonable to assume that in absolute terms the money spent by the young on buying products at the department stores is likely to be higher than that spent by the middle-aged customers. After all, the needs of the young are greater than those of the middle-aged. And so is their income. It is sensible to assume that the middle-aged customer, being closer to his retirement age, would be more restrained in his shopping and would confine his purchases to the bare minimum and the essentials. The extravagant shopping could be the momentary spur of the middle-aged. The young on the other hand would like to fully indulge their shopping fantasies. Having a larger income at their disposal, they are likely to be bigger spendthrifts than the middle-aged customers. Hence it is more than likely that in absolute terms the 20% spent by them in department stores is likely to be higher than the 35% of the middle-aged. A simple illustration will make this absolutely clear. Let us assume that the total amount allocated for retail spending by the middle aged is $100. 35% of this, which is supposed to be spent in the department stores, would then translate into $35. On the other hand the retail-shopping budget of a younger person may be $200. 20% of this will translate into $40. Thus the younger person spends $5 more than the middle-aged person in the department store.

It would therefore be a great folly on the part of the department stores, if, based upon this incorrect reading of the figures, they were to reduce the product lines of the young and replace them with additional product lines of the middle aged. From the above line of reasoning, it is apparent that the young would continue to be the bigger contributors to the success of the department stores even in future. After all, the young enjoy a longer earning span, while the middle-aged will be nearing the end of their earning cycle.

Q18. The following appeared in the editorial column of a daily newspaper.

"Faced with rising deficit levels and mounting losses of state-run enterprises, the government decided to slash the bonus levels of state employees by nearly 50%, at least until such time as the fiscal situation improved. Irked at this, a group of government employees numbering about 1000 took out a protest march to the office of the Governor, demanding a rollback of the order. In all, a total number of nearly 40,000 people are employed by the State. The others did not participate in the march. Since the vast majority of the workers did not take part in the march, it can be concluded that they have no objection to the bonus cut. The small number of workers who did protest may have been instigated by other political parties and in any case their views are not representative of the whole as they are in minority. Hence the State need not pay any heed to their protest."

Discuss how well reasoned is this argument.

A18. The argument is based on the sole premise that the group of 1000 protestors acted on their own and independent of the wishes of the other employees and hence their action is not representative of the sentiments of the vast majority of the State employees who number nearly 40,000 in all.

The editorial has failed to consider the other possibilities that might have an important bearing on the argument. It has to be recognised that the issue of bonus is always a very sensitive matter for all employees. After all they are not directly responsible for the losses suffered by the state undertakings or the prevailing fiscal deficit of the government. Hence they are all bound to feel incensed at the decision of the government to slash their bonus entitlement by 50%. Hence to presume that they wholeheartedly agree with the government proposal and have absolutely no objection to the cut would be to expose one's naiveté.

As to why all the 40,000 employees did not participate in the strike, there could be several explanations. The very first explanation could be that the 1000 employees who actually took part in the protest rally were in fact representing various groups of government employees through mutual consent. It may be highly impractical for all the employees to physically participate in the protest march due to constraints of logistics and age and even gender. Further, many of the government employees are employed in the essential services like water works department, the food supplies department, milk distribution, power generation, and the like. It is not possible for such employees to desert their posts, as that would invite public anger, apart from legal consequences. It is further possible that fearing a law and order problem if a vast number of employees took out a protest

97

march, and that too to the governor's office, the city police may have given permission only to a limited group of no more than 1000 employees to take part in the march.

In view of several such possibilities the editorial has seriously erred in inferring that the government need not pay heed to the protesters as they are not representative of all the government employees.

Even otherwise, a protest, howsoever symbolic and small is to be viewed in all seriousness by those who matter, as it is likely to be an expression of a larger discontent, whether expressed or unexpressed.

The conclusion is that the editorial argument lacks credibility as it has reached conclusions on the basis of only one single factor, while completely ignoring the rest.

Q19. The following was circulated as promotional literature to the restaurant owners in Bay City by the Advertisement Department of The Daily Mirror in an attempt to sell advertisement space in the newspaper:

You can substantially increase your business by advertising in The Daily Mirror. Consider the results of our earlier endeavour. In a special 'EAT-OUT' supplement brought out last month, restaurants were encouraged to list their special menus for the weekend. Here is a sample response: The Cozy Cove reported that customers had to wait for 30 minutes on an average before they could be allotted tables on both the weekend days. The special menus that were advertised sold more than the ordinary ones. When asked by the Hotel supervisors if they had seen the advertisement in the newspaper, nearly 60% of the customers replied in the affirmative. More than half of them said they would return on the next weekend."

Discuss how well reasoned you find the argument.

A19. In an obvious attempt to sell advertisement space to the restaurant owners in Bay City, The Daily Mirror, has provided some juicy statistics to prove that the Cozy Cove did exceptionally well by advertising its special menus for the weekend in their special supplement "EAT-OUT", brought out a month ago.

They have relied upon four main issues to highlight that the restaurant did overwhelmingly well; thanks to the advertisement it placed in the special supplement of The Daily Mirror.

First, it is claimed that customers had to wait for an average of 30 minutes to be allotted their tables on both the weekend days. This by itself is not of much significance. It usually happens that all the hotels are more crowded on the weekends due to family outings. In the absence of specific data, it is to be presumed that this is a regular phenomenon.

Second, it is claimed that the "special weekend menus" listed by the restaurant in their advertisement, sold more than the ordinary menus. In the absence of specific data, this claim also will have to be taken with a pinch of salt. After all, every customer who visits the restaurant is sure to carefully scrutinise the entire menu card before placing the order. It is also probable that the "special menus" for the weekend would have been displayed prominently in the restaurant's menu cards and elsewhere. Hence, to presume that all the people who partook of the special menus were only those who had read the advertisement does not sound rational or plausible.

Third, it is claimed that upon enquiry by the hotel staff, 60% of the customers stated that they had indeed read the advertisement. This however, by itself, does not prove that they had come to visit the restaurant as a consequence thereof. After all, the restaurant presumably was already in business, and several of the guests might have been their regular customers. Further, the remaining 40% who had not read the advertisement obviously had come on their own, without in any way being influenced by the advertisement.

Lastly, more than half of those interviewed stated that they would revisit during the next weekend. This implies that in all probability they belonged to the category of the restaurant's regular customers, who always made it a point to come on the weekends without much bothering about the "special weekend dishes" that the restaurant might choose to serve.

Therefore, a cursory reading of the promotional material of The Daily Mirror reveals that there is not much substance in their claims, and the entire argument is crafted only to book more advertisement space for their newspaper. The argument thus lacks credibility.

Q20. The following appeared as an article in an investment weekly:

Demographic studies have shown that as the life expectancy continues to rise, the percentage of old people in the country continues to increase. This appears to be true, since occupation levels in resort towns have declined dramatically during the last six months. During this period hospitals and health centers in the district have reported significantly more visits by patients, and consequently their room are in greater demand. If you are an investor, it makes better sense to buy shares of Reliable Building Co., who are shortly coming out with their initial public offer to fund the construction of old age homes.

Discuss how well reasoned you find this argument.

A20. In this argument, two totally unrelated developments, occurring however during the same period, have been juggled together to reach a certain conclusion, a process akin to a conjurer's trick. Let us try and unravel the mystery surrounding this exercise.

The first development pertains to the dramatic decline in the occupation levels in resort towns during the last six months. The second pertains to the significantly increased visits by patients to hospitals and health centers in the same district, leading to high demand for the rooms. A cursory reading of the above would immediately reveal that the two developments are as different from each other as night is from day. However, using the survey on demographic studies as efficient bait, the argument very cleverly tries to sell to the reader the suggestion that in such a scenario, he, as an investor should go ahead and purchase shares of Reliable Building Co., who are coming out with an initial public offer to fund the construction of old age homes. Let us consider how compelling is this argument.

In the first development, the occupancy rates at resort towns seem to have fallen dramatically during the last six months. This is being linked to the demographic studies which reveal that as life expectancy continues to rise, the percentage of old people in the country also continues to rise. The obvious conclusion being drawn here is that, with the increase in the older population, the town resorts are becoming increasingly redundant. But is this a valid conclusion? It certainly does not seem so. For one, the dramatic decline in occupancy rates at the resort towns is no more than six months old. After all, this may be just a routine business trend, due to seasonal changes and climatic fluctuations. Resort towns are usually packed during summer, but empty during winter. Therefore, nothing sinister can be read into this simple development. The decline in the rates of occupancy could also mark the end of the holiday season and return of the tourists to their own destinations. It could also be due to some temporary negative factors prevailing there during this period such as water shortages and power cuts, or perhaps outbreak of some disease. It also could be due to a sudden rise in the hotel rental rates due to excessive earlier demand. However, by no stretch of imagination can these be linked to the increasing population of old people in the country. After all, an increase in life expectancy does not automatically mean the automatic extinction of the younger population! And, pray, is there any law, which prevents the elderly from visiting the resort towns for a holiday?

The second development is the sudden rise in the level of patients to hospitals and health centers in the same district, leading to a demand for the available rooms. This again may be due to so many local factors. It is quite possible that there has been an outbreak of any endemic disease. It could also mean that more people have opted to undergo tests and surgeries at this period of time, which may or may not be incidental.

It is also quite possible that due to some major accident or some other natural calamity in the district, more people are streaming into the hospitals for treatment. The possibilities are endless. However it would be quite foolhardy to presume that all the patients visiting the hospitals during this period are only the elderly. Neither is there any specific data to suggest this.

From this, it is quite clear that neither are the two developments connected in any way, nor is there any evidence to suggest that the decline in the occupancy in the resort towns and the flurry of activity in the hospitals and health centers can be directly attributed to the rise in the population of the older people.

Such being the obvious conclusion, the recommendation to the investors to purchase shares of the construction company raising funds to finance old age homes seems to be misplaced and rather motivated. Hypothetically speaking, even if it were proved that the two developments alluded to above are in fact related, there is still nothing to suggest that old people are just waiting to move out of their existing residences into old age homes!

The argument is thus seriously flawed as it is structured on wrong assumptions, mistaken notions, and illogical correlation of available data.

Q21. The Apollo Health Club was opened with much fanfare two years ago. Since then membership levels have shown a steady decline. Recently the management introduced an indoor swimming with heating facilities. Since the usage did not increase significantly, the management has since decided that it would be better to lower membership fees rather than invest in expensive new features. Discuss how well reasoned is this approach.

A21. This argument hinges upon several key assumptions. In the absence of any tangible data regarding the health club, one has to rely upon alternative assumptions to judge the veracity of the argument.

Let us first look at the facts. The Apollo Health Club was formed two years ago with much fanfare, but has seen a steady decline in its membership since then. The moot question is: What could have led to this decline? Let us consider the possibilities one by one.

First, it is quite possible that the club is not properly or conveniently located. It may be located at quite a distance from the main residential or city areas, making it quite cumbersome for members to travel all the way to reach it. In the alternative, it could be situated in a very busy area, and consequently saddled with serious parking problems, making it extremely difficult for members to park their vehicles.

Second, having enrolled for membership enthusiastically at the time of its launch (admittedly with great fanfare), the members may have subsequently realised that it was not adequately equipped. Or, the equipment could be of sub-standard category. There might be a shortage of essential amenities like toilets or bathrooms. There could also be other problems like lack of proper water supply, or frequent breakdown of electricity.

Third, it is also possible that the health club is understaffed or the existing staff members are not properly trained and devoid of any talent. It is quite possible that the critical staff members like trainers, dieticians, and physicians are not properly qualified. It is also quite likely that in the absence of proper supervision from the management, the junior staff are not quite attentive to the needs of the members, or worse, even rude and discourteous.

Fourth, we have to consider the competition factor. It is quite possible that the Apollo Health Club does not measure up to the high standards of the rival clubs in the city and this has led to members opting for the services of its competitors.

Any or a combination of the above factors could have been responsible for the steady decline in the fortunes of the Apollo Health Club since its inception two years ago. If such is actually the case, then a downward revision in the membership fees, as envisaged by the management, will do pretty little to bring the members back. However, if the membership fees are actually perceived to be substantially on the higher side in relation to the amenities offered by it, or in comparison with those charged by its competitors, then a suitable downward reduction in the fees, as envisioned by the management might go a long way in stemming the declining trend in its membership. Therefore the decision of the management will be effective only subject to the fulfillment of this caveat.

However, a silver lining for the Apollo Health Club is apparent from the catchword in the argument, which states that the usage did not "significantly" improve consequent to the opening of the new indoor swimming pool with heating facilities. This indeed is a left-handed compliment for it implies that the usage has in fact improved but not to significant levels. It is just possible then that the absence of a proper swimming pool was one of the major negatives at the club, and with the rectification of this anomaly, members are steadily beginning to come back, though apparently in trickles. This leaves hope for the Apollo Health Club to regain its membership to a great extent with the passage of time, and in such a situation, there is no case for a reduction in fees, particularly since the club will have to bear the additional investment and running costs of the swimming pool.

The argument is thus subject to a lot of assumptions and caveats, and in the absence of proper data, no one line of action can be recommended.

Q22. The following appeared as a recommendation from the General Manager of Ferguson Engineering Products to the Board of Directors:

"It has come to my notice recently that the management of Best Engineering Company has laid off about 25% of their employees in all divisions and at all levels and it is actively encouraging retirement amongst its most senior employees by offering an attractive voluntary retirement package. As our profitability has been declining, we should forthwith hire a significant portion of these employees, as they will bring with them significant experience gained at Ferguson, will require little or no training and also be prepared to work at the same levels of pay drawn by them at Best Engineering. This strategy will be particularly helpful as we also manufacture several products that are being manufactured by them.

Discuss how well reasoned you find this argument.

A22. The available data suggests that the argument is illogical and self-defeating. Let us analyze in detail.

The fact that Best Engineering Company has already laid off about 25% of its workforce spread over all their divisions and at all levels, and is further encouraging retirement amongst its senior employees by offering an attractive voluntary retirement package is a clear indicator of the fact the company is obviously in the process of winding up its present business activity. Apparently it does not find its present operations remunerative or profitable, for whatever reason.

Ferguson Engineering Products on the other hand is in the business of manufacturing several products, which are similar to those manufactured by Best Engineering Company. Of late their profitability has been declining. They hope to rectify this situation, by taking advantage of the layoffs being effected by their rival manufacturer and forthwith hiring a significant number of the laid off employees at pay scales similar to those of Best Engineering Company. They genuinely feel that this strategy will be beneficial to them, since the laid off employees will bring with them rich experience of the rival company, would require little or no training, having worked on similar products earlier, and would also be prepared to work at their earlier pay scales.

This recommendation has been put forth by the General Manager of Ferguson Engineering Products to his Board of Directors. The General Manager has clearly erred in completely misreading the reality of the situation. For one, his company is already running in losses. Secondly the rival company, which is laying off their staff, is also admittedly in the manufacture of a similar line of products. This should have convinced the Manager that the business in which both the companies find themselves in is no longer productive or profitable. While the rival company, clearly reading the signals, is busy obviously winding up its operations, the general manager of Ferguson Engineering Products, on the other hand, is inadvertently trying to compound the problems of his company by attempting to add unnecessary baggage in the form of the laid off employees. This will not only add to the financial burden of a company, already saddled with losses, in the form of additional wages and salaries, but also result in unusually high and perhaps unwanted inventory levels, leading to higher interest and other maintenance expenses.

If the business had been profitable, then the situation would have been altogether different. Additional hiring would have then resulted in higher profitability. However, in that case, the rival manufacturer would not have laid off their employees in the first place. But the very fact that they have in fact done so should have set the alarm bells ringing at Ferguson's.

Hence the argument suffers from a serious misinterpretation of the available data and the business manager at Ferguson Engineering Products would be better advised to do a reality check before implementing his strategy, which is seriously flawed.

Q23. The following is a recommendation from the marketing strategies group of a leading chain stores group to its senior management:

Several clothing and garment stores in our district have reported significantly lower profits for the months of August, September and October. On the other hand stores dealing in home products have reported enhanced profits for the same period. Obviously there is more demand in the market for home products than for clothing and garments. In view of this new trend, wherein it appears that customers are preferring to purchase home products instead of clothing and garments, we should immediately reduce the inventory levels in our clothing and garments department and correspondingly increase the stock in the home furnishings, furniture, and other sundry home products division.

Discuss how well reasoned is this argument.

A23. This argument is flawed because it is based on mistaken assumptions, flowing from an incorrect reading of the available data.

The data suggests that for the months of August, September and October, several clothing and garment stores in the district have reported significantly lower profits, while shops dealing in household products have reported enhanced earnings for the same period. On the basis of this, it is concluded that there is a shift in customer preference for home products as compared to clothing or garments.

The marketing strategies group has obviously failed to take into account the operation of seasonal factors that influence customer sentiment and preferences. It is probable that during the relevant period, there is a normal shift in purchase patterns, which takes place every year. (After all, the period between August and October heralds the arrival of several festivals, concluding with Christmas, and the New Year, which may strongly motivate the people to refurnish and redecorate their homes. As this activity takes quite some time to complete, the required preparations and purchases of the required material have necessarily to be effected some months in advance. This would adequately explain the rise in demand for various home products during those months. However, this trend might again reverse nearer to Christmas and the New Year, when people would again revert to the buying of personal goods like clothing and garments.

Hence, to conclude on the basis of this minor shift in purchase priorities, that there is a major change taking place in the buying habits of the people is to miss the trees for the woods.

The argument is weak and unconvincing.

Q24. The following appeared as a comment in a newspaper editorial:

> The state should continue to provide substantial subsidies to the people on cooking gas, in view of the unbearable rise in the international price of oil. After all, the money thus saved collectively by the households, possibly running into millions of dollars, will find its way into government bonds, which can then be used for funding related activities like coastal oil exploration.

> Discuss how well reasoned you find this argument.

A24. Providing subsidy on cooking gas used for domestic purposes is a populist measure, resorted to, by most governments, in the interests of the common people, and to keep them insulated from the high costs of fuel prevalent in the market. This results in the government absorbing the high financial burden involved therein.

The argument appearing in the editorial strongly advocates this line of action, in view of the 'unbearable rise in the international price of oil.' In an obvious attempt to justify the inevitable drain on the public exchequer that this action will entail, the argument goes on to theorise that the money thus saved by the households through the grant of such subsidies, possibly running into millions of dollars, will ultimately find its way into government bonds, which could then be used for funding related activities like coastal oil exploration. Let us examine the argument critically to see if it is valid.

The available data indicates that the subsidies are substantial in nature, and the international price of oil has risen to unbearable levels. This implies that with every progressive rise in the international price of oil, the financial burden on the government on account of the subsidies, which are admittedly already substantial in nature, goes on escalating to higher levels. If left uncorrected, this mounting burden on the government finances could then seriously impinge on other essential governmental expenditure causing considerable hardships to the people, or even result in an economic disaster for the country as a whole. The government, in order to keep its finances afloat, would then be forced to impose newer and additional taxes on the people, which would then not only fully neutralise the beneficial effect of the existing subsidies, but could ultimately result in casting a much higher burden on the common man.

The other assumption in the argument that the collective amount saved by the households on account of the subsidy, possibly running into several millions of dollars would find its way into government bonds seems to be totally misplaced and overly optimistic. Even though, collectively the money thus saved may run into millions as is being presumed, what is of relevance is the fact that, on a micro level, the overall savings on this account alone, would be too negligible to be considered of any significance whatsoever. And, hypothetically, even assuming that such funds did collectively flow into government bonds, to be finally used for purposes like oil exploration, would the government not have to incur huge interest costs on the money so raised, apart from assuming the responsibility of a crippling debt burden? It would then amount to a classic case of a government munificently gifting its people cash only to borrow it back later from them on interest! Can this be said to be good economics or even good common sense?

The argument is obviously built up on ill-considered assumptions, and is not only illogical, but also irrational.

Q25. The following is a note from the head of research of an investment firm to his marketing team.

In view of the acute scarcity of water in many countries, governments are encouraging the use of rainwater harvesting equipment, for use in domestic and commercial buildings. As a measure to boost the sale of such equipment, our government has also announced a reduction in the sales tax chargeable on it from 6% to just 2%. This will obviously result in great demand for the equipment. ABC Company has just started the manufacture of this wonderful product. In view of the promising future prospects, we should immediately recommend to our clients to buy the shares of this company from the market. Another positive for the company is that Mr. Thomas Mathew, who was till recently on the board of a leading software company, has recently joined the board of this company. The company is sure to benefit from his rich experience.

Discuss how well reasoned is this argument.

A25. The whole argument revolves around the advice sought to be given to investors by the investment firm, to purchase the shares of ABC Company, which is entering the manufacture of rainwater harvesting equipment, and which the investment firm reckons will have good future prospects on this account. Let us consider in depth whether the advice merits attention.

In making his recommendation, the head of research at the investment firm has taken certain factors into consideration. He has obviously been greatly enthused by the future prospects of the rainwater harvesting equipment, which is being actively encouraged by the governments around the world in view of water scarcity in several countries. The fact that our government has announced a reduction on sales tax on this equipment from 6% to just 2% has led the head of the investment firm to seriously believe that there would be a burgeoning market for this kind of equipment in future. However is this assumption justified? Rainwater harvesting equipment, being a relatively new product in the market, and obviously a costly system, is bound to be quite expensive to install. And what would be the real savings on account of this? The water can be harvested only during a relatively good monsoon and in places of acute water scarcity, the level of rainfall is obviously bound to be scanty. Hence the equipment would be lying unused for most part of the year, till the arrival of the rains, when the water could be harvested. How much water could be actually harvested would again depend upon the storage capacity in the building, and the degree of consumption. If the overall savings in water were not considered to be sufficiently high to justify the relatively huge cost of installing and maintaining the equipment, why would the owners of buildings want to purchase it? It might be much cheaper and more convenient to procure the water through water tankers in times of real scarcity.

The other fact is that ABC Company has just launched the manufacture of this equipment. This implies that they are absolutely new to this specific business, and have to build up their marketing from scratch. Launching a brand new product, which is both expensive and untested in the market is no doubt a daunting task. How far they would succeed and at what cost, could be anybody's guess. When there are so many imponderables regarding the new product that is being launched and its manufacturer could there be justification in the recommendation of the investment firm to its investors to invest in such a venture by buying the shares of such a company? Surely not! And in any case, most certainly not on the basis of Mr. Thomas Mathew joining the board of the new company. After all according to the available information, he was an erstwhile director in a software company. Pray, what kind of 'rich experience' can a former director of a software company bring to bear on a company, which proposes to go into the manufacture of rainwater harvesting equipment?

The whole argument appears illogically conceived, without a proper appreciation of the facts and built up on fallacious assumptions.

Q26. The following appeared in the editorial columns of a newspaper: "Governments are giving more and more importance to the farm sector. Huge governmental funds are spent on giving various subsidies to the farmers for purchasing fertilizers, seeds, farm equipment and the like. In many countries, power is supplied free to the farmers. All this is bound to have serious repercussions on the government finances. Further, the supply of food grains is in abundance at present. In fact, food storage sheds are overfull and there is no place left to store further grain. Also, food expenses account for only a small portion of the rising real incomes of the people. The demand for food does not rise in proportion with the rise in real incomes. Yet the government keeps spending substantial amounts on food subsidies and agricultural research. This should be stopped in view of the fiscal deficit." Discuss how well reasoned you find this argument.

A26. There are several issues to this argument. Let us examine them one by one.

The first issue is of farm subsidies per se. It is an undisputed fact that food is not only the lifeline of an individual, but also of a country. A country, which suffers from chronic food shortages and cannot provide sufficient grain to its people, is a very poor country indeed. It will then have to depend on costly and backbreaking import of food items from other countries, resulting in a wasteful drain on its precious foreign resources. Therefore, governments around the world ensure abundance of food grain in their countries by giving sufficient incentives to their farmers in the form of various subsidies and concessions relating to water, power and other resources. Substantial amounts of funds are also earmarked and spent on agricultural research and education, in an attempt to improve farm practices, maximise output, and improve the general quality of the crops grown. This not only benefits the farmers, but also the entire community. People are assured of food grains at affordable cost and in the quantities required. Thus, the argument that the money so spent is bound to have serious repercussions on governmental finances is short sighted and myopic. In the absence of this allocation to the farm sector, valuable resource might have to be spent on importing food grains. In the former instance, money remains within the country, while in the latter case, precious foreign exchange leaves the country's shores. Therefore, this argument is totally misplaced.

The second objection to the farm subsidies stems from the fact that food grains are in abundance at present and the buffer stock is overflowing with grain, with no further place left to store. It would be worthwhile considering if this indeed would have been the case but for the thoughtful subsidies being given to the farm sector. In the immediate context it could be on account of a bountiful harvest in the current year, leading to excessive supply of grain. This again could be used fruitfully as an export opportunity to earn foreign exchange. The argument has obviously failed to comprehend the fact that the surplus in food grain is on account of the subsidies and not in spite of it.

The third objection pertains to the 'small' amount spent on food as a percentage of the rising real incomes of people. This again is due to the fact that food is in abundance thanks to the subsidies and other concessions given to the farm sector. It is also in no small measure due to the investment in agricultural research and education. But for this, the allocation for food in the domestic budget might have sliced off a big chunk from the family income. That sure is for 'real'!

The argument is thus built up on assumptions that are inconsistent with economic realities and thus merits no consideration whatsoever.

Q27. Following appeared in an editorial in a city newspaper:

> The construction of multiplexes and shopping malls during the last two years has seriously affected the civic life of the city. Pollution has gone up because of the increased traffic to the city, there are frequent traffic jams on the city's main roads, and the residents are having difficulties in finding parking space for their cars when they go out shopping. This is not all. Land rates are going up and so is the cost of vegetables and fruit. Since the owners of the malls and multiplexes are obviously raking in huge profits, they should be asked to pay additional taxes to provide extra amenities in the city and widen the city roads. After all, the congestion that the city is witnessing is because of them. Discuss how well reasoned you find this argument.

A27. The editorial has advanced several reasons, in its attempt to substantiate its stand that the construction of multiplexes and shopping malls in the city in the last two years is directly responsible for the several civic problems faced by the city, and its demand that the owners of these buildings should be asked to pay additional taxes for providing extra amenities to the beleaguered populace and also to widen the city roads. Let us critically examine if there is any justification to its stand and the reasons advanced.

The blanket statement that the construction of multiplexes and shopping malls has seriously affected the civic life of the city looks rather far stretched and unconvincing. This is sought to be proved by identifying the problems being faced by the city at present.

It is stated that pollution levels have gone up due to the increase of the traffic to the city. In the absence of other relevant data, this assumption cannot be taken at face value. The increased pollution could also be due to the setting up of more industries in the city and the resultant flow of heavy vehicles transporting goods and materials. It could be due to the open burning of garbage dumps within the city limits. The heavy flow of traffic could also be due to the opening of some national highway connecting the city to the rest of the country. Thus, these two factors by themselves do not in any way prove that they are the result of the opening of the shopping malls and multiplexes in the city.

It is further stated that there are frequent traffic jams on the city's roads and the residents have difficulty in finding parking places when they go out shopping. This argument would have some relevance if it were known for certain that the malls and multiplexes were all located on the same road, or even in the same vicinity. However in the absence of this information, we have to assume that the traffic jams on the road could just be part of natural city phenomena, as the problems of finding parking space in a bustling city are.

It is also stated that the prices of land are going up, and so are the prices of vegetables and fruits. Though this is usually the case in a place where there is a flurry of building activity, it is hard to pinpoint the multiplexes and malls alone as the likely culprits. As for fruits and vegetables, the prices of these commodities are subject to daily fluctuations, depending upon factors of cultivation and demand and supply. It is quite inappropriate to link their rise in prices to the construction of malls and multiplexes!

Having made a complete memo of charges, the editorial goes on to make the outrageous demand that the owners of the malls and multiplexes be asked to pay additional taxes for providing extra amenities to the residents and widening the roads. This makes it sound as if the owners of these commercial complexes have committed some monstrous crime against the city for which they should be punished, and the city folk compensated. What a spurious and phony argument indeed! The owners of the malls and multiplexes should be rightly seen to have done a service to the citizens of the city by risking their resources to build super commercial structures for them. Viewed positively, this has acted as a wealth creator for the people in the form of enhanced land prices for the owners of land. The heightened commercial activity generated by these complexes would be a source of additional employment for several of the city's unemployed. The educated and technically qualified could find lucrative opportunities for bettering their job prospects. Finally, the city's shoppers would enjoy a shopping bonanza.

As for the funds required for providing additional amenities and widening roads, the local government should be only too happy to oblige, considering the additional revenues that would be flowing into its coffers on account of the newfound economic growth straddling the city.

The argument, on the whole is hollow, built up on misconceived grounds, and devoid of any real merit.

Q28. The following is a recommendation made to the Managing Director of a leading Travel Group specialising in organising foreign holidays from the Group's marketing manager:

A recent survey on tourist behaviour found that most travelers going abroad, especially the first timers, spent a good deal of their time and money on visiting diverse hotels and restaurants, serving foods of different countries. It appears then, that most people who go abroad do so to taste exotic international dishes. In order to capitalise on this trend, we should immediately promote an intercontinental food court in this city of international standards. This will be frequently patronised not only by the regular foreign travelers, but also those who are poor and cannot afford to go on holiday abroad.

Discuss how well reasoned you find this argument.

A28. "If you cannot go to the world, the world will come to you." This sums up in a nutshell the pet theme of this argument.

On the basis of a recent survey on tourist behaviour, it was found that most travelers going abroad spent a good deal of their time and money on eating exotic international foods in a cross section of restaurants and hotels. On the basis of this, it is surmised that most travelers who travel abroad, go with the main intention of feeding on exotic international dishes. This 'realisation' has so tickled the taste buds of the marketing manager that he has made a rather startling recommendation to his managing director to immediately launch an intercontinental food court of international standards to pander to the city's populace.

Amusing as the suggestion may be, let us try and rationalise his decision.

At the outset, however, it must be affirmed that his assumption that people go abroad mainly to tickle their palate is not credible. Who would spend a small fortune going abroad just to taste some exotic dishes? It is another thing that once there, the travelers have to eat, and here they would rather be adventurous! But to surmise that eating is their prime motive in going abroad is being ludicrous.

If this were to be accepted, then it follows that the prospects of a food court, that too serving expensive intercontinental would be rather uncertain. This is not to question the business prospects of such a venture per se, but purely on the premise that it will be patronised by all those who travel abroad. As for enticing the poor who cannot afford to travel abroad to enjoy these delicacies, it is to be presumed that they would still be too poor to afford the luxury of such expensive fare even on home turf.

The argument is thus illogically conceived and more amusing than convincing. Not a shred of hard evidence has been advanced to substantiate the logic behind the argument, except fanciful conjecturing.

Q29. The following appeared as a letter to the Editor of a daily:

> The city council's decision to build a flyover at the busy Main Square should be resisted by the local residents tooth and nail, as this will entail demolishing several old buildings, which were constructed several decades ago and thus have historical significance. Granted that accidents do often happen at this point due to chaotic traffic conditions, but this is not reason enough to demolish ancient buildings that add historical flavour to this city, and bring in the tourists. Instead some other way should be found to manage the traffic.

> Discuss how well reasoned is this argument.

A29. The letter to the editor of a city daily strongly exhorts the city's residents to fight tooth and nail, the city council's decision to build a flyover at the busy Main Square, notwithstanding the accidents caused by the chaotic traffic conditions, which it is quick to acknowledge. The bone of contention is in the decades-old and ancient buildings, which will have to be demolished if the flyover is to be constructed. These are said to have historical value and help to attract tourists. Let us see how well reasoned this argument is.

First, the urgent and compelling reason for building the flyover at the busy square seems to be the frequent accidents taking place there due to the chaotic traffic conditions. This much is an admitted fact. On the other hand, the call to the people to fight this initiative of the city council is ostensibly to save the ancient and decades old buildings that will have to be demolished in the process. The justification given for saving these structures is that being ancient buildings, they add historical flavour to the city and invite tourists. The point to consider is whether this justification provides reason enough to abort the public interest initiative of the city council. On the one hand, at stake is the life and limb of the populace, while on the other is the aesthetic urge of an over zealous individual to preserve the supposed flavour of history in the city and attract tourists. Logic clearly dictates that in a tradeoff between the two, the former should prevail. Pray, of what use is history if a man does not live to appreciate it? As for tourists, none would want to visit the city, if they have to pay for the pleasure with their life or limb.

The argument is thus hollow, devoid of logic and built up on pure sentiment and zeal. A classic case of the heart ruling the head.

Q30. The following was a suggestion from the managing director of Telematics, manufacturing hi-tech communication equipment for satellite purposes: "Ever since we decentralised our manufacturing operations some years ago, our profitability has declined. We should therefore revert to our earlier model, by closing some of our assembly lines and shifting them to a large central plant. Cape town would be the best choice for this. Employee wages have been consistently low here, and there is a surplus labour force available due to the closure of some loss making industries in the recent past. Apart from these obvious advantages, the local council has agreed to provide us government land at lower cost and waive taxes for the first five years of operations. What more can we ask for?" Discuss how well reasoned you find this argument.

A30. The managing director of Telematics, has suggested the closing down of some of their assembly lines and shifting them to a large central plant, on the assumption that the earlier decentralisation of manufacturing operations has resulted in declined profitability of the company. For this purpose, he feels that Cape Town would be the best choice. He has based his preference for Cape Town on three parameters. Let us analyze all three to understand if the argument is credible or not.

At the outset, it needs to be emphasised that his assumption that the profitability of the company has declined due to the earlier decentralisation of operations is not very convincing. No data has been provided to substantiate such an assumption. Any number of factors could have been responsible for the declining profitability. It could be due to adverse business conditions, higher competition in the market, rise in the cost of raw materials, increased interest burden or even bad debts. In the absence of specific figures, no presumptions can be made.

As to the choice of Cape Town for shifting his operations, one of the reasons he has advanced to justify his choice, is that the wages of employees here have been consistently low. While this may appear to be advantageous on the surface, a deeper reading of the situation may reveal that it is not actually so. Consistently lower wages may mean that the employees are not suitably skilled or qualified. It could also mean that the general productivity of the employees here is not up to the mark. It may also mean that many of them are raw and inexperienced.

The second reason advanced is that there is a surplus of labour force available here due to the closure of some loss-making industries in the recent past. This perhaps better explains the phenomenon of consistent low wages earned by the employees here. One will also have to delve deep into the reasons for the losses made by the industries that have closed down, as no relevant data has been provided. Perhaps it is due to the poor quality of the labour available here. Perhaps it is due to other unfavourable factors prevalent here like poor infrastructure, scarcity of raw materials, water shortage, power shortage and poor law and order situation, leading to frequent thefts and robberies. If some or a majority of these factors are found to actually exist, then the choice of Cape Town on the strength of the first two reasons analyzed above immediately raises a question mark.

The third reason advanced is the waiver of taxes for the first five years of operations by the City Council and provision of government land at lower cost. This in fact, compounds the suspicion that all is not well with Cape Town. This concession by the City Council exhibits desperation at the state of affairs prevailing in the town. How else can one explain the decision to waive taxes for a period of five years, when the attempt should actually be to try and raise additional resources to develop the town?

The three reasons, taken together, paint a rather gloomy picture for the prospects of industry in this town. That the managing director of a company manufacturing hi-tech communications equipment for satellite purposes, which would require extremely skilled and qualified manpower for their operations, should have thought it fit to set up a centralised plant in this town raises serious doubts about the reasoning involved in his decision-making. The very factors, which should have appeared negative even at first glance, have been viewed positively, leading to an extremely unsound judgment. An extremely illogical thought process indeed.

Q31. At a meeting of the business strategies group of a leading ice-cream maker to identify newer outlets for the company's products, the following remark was made by a member:

We should not consider opening a retail ice-cream parlour in Snow Town. The winters there are quite cold, which will adversely affect our sales. Although the other months enjoy normal climate, many tourists frequent the city during the winter months because of the winter sports. Hence we will not be able to capitalise on the tourist potential. Further, it has come to my notice that the only other ice-cream shop in the city, which is being operated by our rival manufacturer has seen a 10% dip in sales this winter, in spite of the fact that the town has a population of nearly 12,000 people and there is no other ice-cream shop anywhere in the vicinity.

Discuss how well reasoned you find this argument.

A31. The reasons advanced for not opening an ice-cream parlor in Snow Town are not credible or convincing. It appears that the available data has not been properly evaluated or analysed. Let us consider all the facts.

The argument rests on the prime assumption that cold winters in Snow Town do no augur well for the sales of ice cream in this town. However a closer reading of the available data indicate otherwise. The available facts indicate that many tourists frequent this town in the months of winter due to the winter sports. Therefore, there is no reason why there should be any doubt regarding the sales of ice cream even during winter. Indeed, there is ample corroboration provided by the fact that the ice-cream parlour run by the rival manufacturer does record sales in the months of winter, though it is stated that the sales this time are lower by about 10%. This in itself is a positive sign. A margin of just 10% is an acceptable figure for volume fluctuations in sales.

The available data also states that apart from winter, the other months in the year experience normal climate. There is then no reason, whatsoever, why the ice-cream parlour should not do good business, when the town is admittedly a tourist destination.

Apart from this fact, it is stated that the town has a population of 12,000 people and only one shop to serve ice cream. This by itself should be viewed as a huge positive. The competition would come from just one other shop selling ice cream. The fact that there is no other ice cream parlour anywhere in the vicinity should ensure ample market for both the rival players to co-exist. In fact, it is generally acknowledged that the arrival of competition stirs more interest and a better quality product comes forth due to increased publicity by the various players, leading to the creation of an enhanced market for it. This then benefits all the players.

It would appear that the argument advanced is not fully based upon proper appreciation of the existing data.

Q32. The following was a report by the CEO of a leading manufacturing company to his Board of Directors:

I have learnt from the morning newspapers that Popular Automobile Co. that has just moved into our state is offering to hire people at salaries that are nearly 50% higher than those paid by us to our experienced employees. In addition it is offering higher annual bonus. We should forthwith increase the salaries paid to our employees to bring them on par with those offered by the new entrant. Otherwise we may lose a sizeable number of our employees to them, and this will seriously affect our operations. Already there are reports that some of our employees have left to work for them.

Discuss how well reasoned you find this argument.

A32. The CEO of the leading manufacturing company is clearly rattled by the arrival in his state of Popular Automobile Co. which is offering to hire people at salaries that are nearly 50% higher than those paid by them to their experienced employees, in addition to higher annual bonus. He expects to prevent likely attrition from his company by giving matching salaries to his staff. Let us analyze how well reasoned his decision-making is.

It is well to note that the other manufacturer is moving into the same state and not into the same city or town where the existing manufacturer is located. For all we know, the rival manufacturers could be located hundreds of miles apart. If such is indeed the case, then we can safely assume that not all the employees, if at all any, will opt to relocate to a new location, in unfamiliar surroundings. Even if they so opt, they will have to take into account the additional expenses involved for lodging and boarding and transportation. It is quite possible that the additional 50% being offered by Popular Automobile Co. may not be enough to adequately compensate them for these additional expenses. It is also possible that the company is located in some obscure and forlorn place, which may prove to be a stumbling block for the prospective employees.

Another relevant fact pertains to the type of products manufactured by the two companies. The new entrant is obviously a manufacturer of automobiles or related items, but the products manufactured by the existing company have not been disclosed in the proposition. If the manufacturing activity of the two companies is totally unrelated as far as the product is concerned, then the fear of migration of employees from one to the other is totally unfounded, because each manufacturing process will demand different skill sets.

The fact that only a few employees have actually migrated to the other company seems to support the above observation. It is possible that the employees who have actually migrated, belong to the office and clerical segment, and are in no way connected to the manufacturing activity. If so, then they can be very easily replaced, without resort to additional pay.

Therefore, for a credible assessment of the problem, it is vital to identify the product manufactured by the existing company. This alone would hold the key to any future course of action. The course of action enunciated by the CEO would be justified only if it is known for certain that both the companies are same product rivals, and that too after a proper assessment of other considerations discussed herein. Otherwise, the additional burden of a substantial pay-hike would not only have been in vain, but also with accompanying risks of seriously jeopardising the profitability of the company in the long run.

Therefore the argument can be said to be logically valid only under specific circumstances.

Q33. The following article appeared in a weekly shoppers magazine:

Shopkeepers of general merchandise in New City complain that they have been badly hit by the recent advent of mail order and Internet shopping. Even shopping malls are reporting losing business in this fashion. The goods ordered are promptly delivered within 24 hours by courier vans or Quick mail service. A positive outcome of this new trend is that shoppers no longer need to drive around the city to various shops to buy their requirements. This will, no doubt, result in saving of substantial vehicle fuel in New City and also reduce the traffic congestion on the city roads.

Discuss how well reasoned you find the argument.

A33. There are two aspects to this argument.

The first assumes that shopkeepers of general merchandise and even shopping malls are badly affected by the advent of mail order and Internet shopping. Though this is likely to be true to a certain extent, yet the statement sounds a little exaggerated. After all, everything cannot be ordered over the Internet and everything cannot be procured through mail order. After all one cannot try out a pair of trousers on the Internet. Nor can one procure a jar of pickles through mail order. Hence the sweeping statement that shoppers no longer need to drive around city roads to buy their requirements needs to be taken with a pinch of salt. It is possible that the declining business volumes at the stores and supermarkets are a normal business phenomenon, but for want for anything more specific to lay the blame on, the shopkeepers have turned their ire upon mail order and Internet!

The second and more hilarious aspect of this argument propounds the theory that as a result of the new trend, there will be substantial saving of fuel in the city and that the city's roads will see lesser traffic congestion. If such were really the case, any government would quickly sit up and take notice, for this bit of discovery would undoubtedly be sweet music to its ears! It would also greatly gladden the hearts of harried town planners who often have to cope with the nightmare of unending traffic snarls on the city roads, and receive no sympathy from the citizens for their woes.

Does it need a genius to theorise that many a time shopping is but an excuse for people to go out on a drive? And if there is no shopping, there is no stopping either! The traffic will only move in another direction. But the roads will never be deserted. Ever. No one needs to worry on that account. And if at all the city will save fuel because of the customer not visiting the storekeeper, the delivery van of the courier or the local mail vehicle will quickly move in to restore the balance by coming to the doorstep of the customer.

On a serious note, the argument is highly flawed because it has relied more upon wild speculation and fancy conjectures rather than hard rationale.

Q34. The following appeared as a contribution from a reader in a weekly health magazine.

It is well known that milk and other dairy products are rich in Calcium and Vitamin D, which are essential for the healthy growth and maintenance of bones. As osteoporosis is a disorder, often linked to hereditary factors, in which the bones in the body tend to substantially weaken with age, it is commonly believed that a diet rich in milk and dairy products helps prevent it. However, a long-term study of a large segment of people showed that those who had consistently consumed milk and dairy products throughout the years of study suffered from a higher rate of bone fractures than the other participants in the study. Since bone fractures are normally associated with osteoporosis, the study results indicate that a prolonged consumption of dairy products may actually increase, not decrease the disorder.

Discuss how well reasoned you find this argument.

A34. This argument is partly based on common myths and partly on facts. Let us consider both in order to determine whether the argument is credible.

First, the facts. It is a medically accepted fact that milk and other dairy products are rich in Calcium and Vitamin D, which are essential elements in the healthy growth of bones and other hard tissues in the body. It is also recognised that osteoporosis is a disorder of the bones, often linked to hereditary factors, resulting in the weakening of the bones with age. This leads to brittleness of the bones making them vulnerable to frequent fractures and cracks.

Next, the myths. It is commonly believed that an intake of milk and dairy products prevents osteoporosis. If we match myth with fact, we will know what the actual reality is. The data clearly states that osteoporosis is often linked to hereditary factors. This implies that the disorder is independent of the consumption of milk and other dairy products. It then follows that if the weakness of the bones were to be due just to a dietary deficiency of milk and dairy products, it would not be classified as osteoporosis, but as a general problem occurring on account of insufficient intake of Calcium and Vitamin D. In such a case, the obvious remedy would be to enhance the intake of products rich in the above substances, including milk and other dairy products. Thus it follows that osteoporosis cannot be directly linked to the deficiency of milk and other dairy products. It may then be surmised that osteoporosis is not on account of deficiency of milk and other dairy products, but in spite of them.

Let us now consider the results of the study conducted. The long-term study is reported to have found that those who had consistently consumed milk and other dairy products throughout the period of such study, suffered from a higher rate of bone fractures than all other participants in the study. From this it was concluded that a prolonged intake of milk and other dairy products actually increased the disorder and not decreased it.

It should be noted that there is no data to indicate the actual criteria applied to choose the participants of the study. It is unclear whether the people chosen actually suffered from osteoporosis or not. It was just concluded that people who had consistently consumed milk and other dairy products throughout the period of the study, suffered a higher rate of fractures than all the other participants. This could be purely incidental, in which case not much importance can be attached to the findings. After all, fractures are a common occurrence due to falls or other common accidents and are not the result of osteoporosis alone. It has never been medically affirmed that those who consume milk or other dairy products will never ever suffer fractures.

The fallacy in this argument is that it has linked bone fractures to osteoporosis. The discussion above shows that this assumption is totally misplaced and wrong. Fractures per se cannot prove the presence of osteoporosis. They are only a symptom of the disorder, not the disorder itself. Hence the conclusion that a consistent intake of milk and other dairy products increases the disorder and does not decrease it is patently flawed. In fact no such conclusion can be reached either way because fractures by themselves do not confirm the presence or absence of osteoporosis in a person.

The argument is thus totally flawed and illogical, based as it is, more on myths than facts.

Q35. The following is a hurried memo from the marketing manager of a packaged foods company.

"The recent study (results published in the latest edition of Medical Miracles) conducted on the inhabitants of Seaview, accidentally stumbled on a rather startling discovery. It was found that the people living in this town where fish consumption is very high visited the doctor only once or twice in a year for the treatment of common colds. Further, there were hardly any cases of viral fever recorded, even though the neighbouring district reported a high incidence of such cases. This proves that regular consumption of fish can prevent colds, and cure viral infections. As we are in the business of packaged foods, we should immediately replace meat products with fish products. The publication of this report is sure to boost our business, if we do so." Discuss how well reasoned is this argument.

A35. The survey has concluded that regular consumption of fish can prevent colds and cure viral infections, because the inhabitants of Seaview, where there is a high consumption of fish, visit the doctor only once or twice a year for colds and reportedly faced no attack of viral fever even though the neighbouring district had a high incidence of it. Is this a rational and logical conclusion? Let us analyze.

It is common knowledge that colds are the outcome of viral infections, and are generally caused by water-borne bacteria. The occurrence of common colds is particularly high during the rainy season when there are more chances of drinking water getting contaminated, due to overflowing drains and sewers. Viral fevers are also generally caused in this way. It is common knowledge that there is no curative treatment for common colds. Only symptomatic treatment is prescribed. Colds generally last only for a few days and few people, if any, take the trouble to go to a doctor for specific treatment, barring more severe cases of infection. Most pharmacists dispense medication for common colds and fever across the counter, and normally it is no more than analgin and paracetamol tablets. This then probably accounts for the fact that the residents of Seaview go to the doctor only once or twice for cases of common cold. In fact, this period might actually coincide with the onset of the monsoon rains. There is absolutely nothing strange or bizarre about it.

Further, it is also possible that the residents of Seaview have a highly efficient system of drinking water distribution, which minimises the chances of its contamination even during the rainy season. It is also possible that a majority of the residents use water filtration systems in their homes.

Hence, by no stretch of imagination can it be concluded, purely on the basis of the above argument that the eating of fish prevents the occurrence of common colds and cures viral fevers. No medical research data in this field has been advanced to justify such a claim. Perhaps, if the residents of Seaview were prone to eating more meat, then meat eating would have been declared to be the preventive factor for colds!

Thus the argument is irrational, and devoid of any logic.

Q36. Opinion polls conducted by a leading agency in all the major cities across the country had concluded that the ruling United Democratic Party, which has been consistently pro-reform, would sweep the polls. After all, there is a boom in the country's stock markets, land prices are soaring, industry is flourishing, and taxes have been significantly lowered on restaurants and bars serving liquor. However, in a major upset, the rival Peoples Party, which hardly has any urban base, but promised to benefit farmers, and adopt labour friendly policies if it is voted to power, actually won the elections by a huge margin. This proves that opinion polls are not a true reflection of the people's desires, or perhaps people will not correctly divulge their choices before the actual elections.

Discuss how well reasoned you find this argument.

A36. The argument is based on an election upset, in which the United Democratic Party, which was also the ruling party, was expected to sweep the polls, lost to the rival Peoples Party, by a huge margin. This was also contrary to the opinion polls conducted by a leading agency, which had predicted a big win for the former. Hence, it is surmised that opinion polls are not a true reflection of the people's desires or possibly the people will not correctly divulge their true choices before the actual election. Let us analyze the facts to ascertain which of the two conclusions reached is correct, or whether they are both wrong.

The facts state that the incumbent United Democratic Party was consistently pro-reform. This reflected in a stock market boom, soaring land prices, and a flourishing industry. Taxes were also reportedly reduced on restaurants and bars serving liquor. It is obvious that the main beneficiaries of the pro-reformist actions would have been the urban elite, who live in large cities and towns and have the wherewithal to trade on the stock exchanges, are rich enough to own lands, and prosperous enough to visit restaurants and bars serving liquor. This would also include the wealthy industrialists whose businesses were also reportedly flourishing.

On the other hand the rival Peoples Party with a pro-poor leanings promised to benefit the farmers and the labour classes if voted to power. The beneficiaries in this case would be the vast chunk of rural masses who depend on agriculture for their livelihood, and the huge army of industrial labour spread far and wide in the countryside and the smaller towns and hamlets. It would also encompass the other working classes who depend on fixed salaries or daily wages for their sustenance. The booming stock markets and the soaring land prices would be of little consequences to the fortunes of these less privileged.

But why did the opinion polls go wrong? After all that is the million-dollar question. The data states that the opinion polls were conducted in all the major cities of the country. Therein perhaps lies the real answer. Apparently overawed by the prevailing economic boom and the expectations that the ruling dispensation would return with a sweeping majority, the pollsters obviously confined themselves only to the major cities across the country, and to interviewing only those sections of the society, which had been the biggest beneficiaries of the benign policies of the ruling clique. And this proved to be their undoing. They were blissfully unaware of the winds of change sweeping across the larger countryside and the remote towns and villages, because they did not care to go there.

Q37. A recent medical survey showed that people who lived in apartment blocks having elevators suffered from more heart problems than people who lived in buildings, which had only stairs, and no elevators. It was also found that the elderly residents of apartment block with elevators, paid twice as many visits to their doctors as did people of the buildings with elevators. The obvious conclusion based on these findings is that the moderate amount of exercise involved in routinely using the staircase helps to avert heart problems and also ensures better health for the elderly residents. Based on these findings, city builders would be better advised to construct buildings without elevators, as those would be preferred more by the people, in order to remain healthier.

Discuss how well reasoned you find this argument.

A37. This argument is based on the sole assumption, that the moderate level of exercise involved in routinely using the staircase in the normal course, helps to avert heart problems in people, and also ensures better health for the elderly residents. Let us see if the assumption is valid.

The assumption itself is primarily based on the results of a medical survey, which showed that people who lived in buildings with elevators suffered more heart problems than people who lived in buildings with only staircases but no elevators. This sweeping conclusion reportedly based on a medical survey, however, has not advanced any credible medical data to substantiate its validity. There is no mention of the methodology used and the exact results obtained to justify such a conclusion. Nor is there any mention of the background of the participants who took part in the survey. In the absence of such information it is impossible to establish the veracity of the findings. It is quite likely that a larger number of people who are already faced with heart problems would naturally opt for apartments in a block with elevators, while others without such compulsions would have no hesitation in opting for ones without elevators. In such a scenario the results would be absolutely meaningless. The results would have some meaning only if people developed heart problems only after coming to reside in the blocks having elevators. Therefore, the truth of the findings would be subject only to such a condition.

On the other hand, it is stated that elderly residents in elevator blocks pay visits to doctors twice the number of times as those who live in only-staircase blocks. This again may be a self-fulfilling argument. The elderly who are fortunate to live in elevator blocks, would naturally find it much more convenient to pay more visits to their doctor than the others, who would be forced to undertake the arduous climb of their staircases, in which situation they would be inclined to reduce the number of visits to their doctor. This then, would not automatically imply that they are any healthier than their elevator-block brethren. It may also mean that instead of visiting their doctor, perhaps the doctor would come to visit them at home.

Hence the argument is rather weak and unconvincing. Had there been clinching medical evidence, perhaps, the argument would have sounded more credible, but in its absence, it sounds rather hollow.

Q38. The following appeared in the editorial of a daily newspaper.

> In view of the rising incidence of accidents involving two-wheelers, the government had promulgated a law a year ago, making the wearing of helmets compulsory. However, statistics reveal that there has actually been an increase in the accidents involving two-wheelers in the last twelve months. It appears that helmets lull the motorcyclists into a false sense of complacency, making them more reckless on the roads. Therefore the law regarding compulsory wearing of helmets should be revoked immediately in order to bring down the accident rate. Discuss how well reasoned is this argument.

A38. The argument assumes that the wearing of helmets lulls the motorcyclists into a false sense of complacency, making them more reckless on the roads. This factor is being linked to the increased accident rate in the last twelve months since the wearing of helmets was made compulsory. Let us analyze if the assumption is valid.

While making this assumption, the argument has conveniently overlooked the other factors that could have led to the rising rate of accidents since the wearing of helmets was made compulsory. It is quite probable that the accidents were due to the recklessness and negligence of the other motorists on the road. The argument assumes that the motorcyclists might have become more reckless, as a result of the wearing of the helmets. Is this likely? After all, in any accident the two-wheeler rider is more vulnerable to serious injury, even live-threatening at times, than is the driver of a four-wheeler. There is no scarcity of cases when innocent riders of two wheelers have had to pay with their life or limb for the misdeeds on the roads of drivers of other bigger vehicles like buses and trucks, who revel in overtaking each other.

Another factor contributing to the rise in the accidents could also be poor infrastructure, in the form of bad roads, poor lighting, bad or faulty signals, and a poor enforcement of traffic rules. Bad roads with cracks or potholes are particularly death traps for the unwary motorcyclists. Hence, any number of reasons could be responsible for the rising graph of accidents, and to put the blame on helmets for the rising accidents is akin to blaming the bulletproof jacket of a soldier for his death! Hence the assumption is illogical and irrational.

As for the suggestion to revoke the law on compulsory wearing of helmets to bring down the accident rate, it is again akin to asking the army to lay down arms before the enemy on the battlefield in order to win the battle. In any case, it needs to be understood, that the purpose behind the wearing of helmets could never be to prevent the accidents per se, but to avert serious and life threatening injury to the wearer. In a situation of rising accidents, the law needs to be enforced even more stringently.

The argument is thus baseless and totally irrational.

Q39. The following appeared in the editorial of a local daily.

> Five years ago, the local authorities built a subway plaza in the busy commercial area near the main railway terminus. As business continued to grow since then, and with the plaza becoming more and more congested, construction was started last year on another subway plaza in the vicinity. However, due to sudden paucity of funds, the project has slowed down in the last few months. In the meantime, the city council has sanctioned additional funds for the building of a six-story parking garage near the rail terminus in order to increase the parking space in the area and reduce severe congestion on the main parking bay on the road. However, in view of the scarcity of resources, the available funds should first be spent on the completion of the new subway plaza. When this is completed, business will flourish even more and ultimately bring in much higher revenues to the government in the form of taxes. These tax revenues can then be used to conveniently fund the construction of the multi-storied parking garage.

> Discuss how well reasoned is this argument.

A39. The argument poses the classic million-dollar question: What came first, the chicken or the egg? Let's find out.

It is suggested that the funds being sanctioned for the construction of six-story parking garage near the rail terminal, in order to reduce the severe congestion on the main parking bay on the road, be instead diverted towards the completion of the second subway plaza, where work has reportedly slowed down in the last few months due to a paucity of resources. Is this a credible suggestion? The available data indicates that there is an impending urgency for building the parking garage in view of the absolute congestion on the main parking bay on the road and also to increase the parking space to meet the enhanced demand from the escalating number of vehicles. This might have been rendered inevitable by the construction of the first subway plaza five years ago, which has since become much congested, necessitating the construction of a second. If the funds were to be diverted, instead, for completing the construction of the second subway plaza, what then would be the solution to the vexed problem of the severe congestion faced at the main parking bay on the road?

The argument goes on to suggest that the successful completion of the second subway plaza will see business flourishing even more, culminating in higher revenues for the government, in the form of additional taxes, which could then be used to conveniently fund the multistoried parking garage. The argument is rather specious, as it does not factor in the explosive situation that would arise with regard to the parking of vehicles, upon completion of the second plaza. The existing severe congestion on the main parking bay on the road near the rail terminus, is likely to get further compounded, many times over, by the time the second plaza is completed, and thereafter the situation would in all likelihood turn truly uncontrollable with the additional vehicles headed for the second plaza fighting for parking space. This unruly and unmanageable situation could then lead to frequent law and order problems, apart from posing serious traffic hazards. Such undesirable fallout could then adversely impact businesses in both the plazas leading to a gradual decline in revenues to the government. This would then turn out to be a self-defeating exercise. Even otherwise, if the construction of the multistoried parking plaza were to be held hostage to the generation of adequate tax revenues from the two plazas, it is quite possible that the parking complex might never ever see the light of dawn. The construction of public infrastructure is always capital intensive and can never be linked to the generation of any specified source of current income, which may or may not materialise, for fructification.

The argument is thus illogical and unconvincing. Obviously, construction of the parking garage must take precedence over the completion of the second subway plaza.

Q40. The following appeared in the latest monthly issue of 'Animal Lovers'.

A recent survey has revealed that those who own pets lead happier and healthier lives than people who do not have pets. This was found to be so more in the case of people who owned dogs. Such people suffered less from heart problems than the others and hardly had to visit their doctor. Heart patients who do not have a dog, would then do well to adopt one immediately. In this way they can avoid frequent trips to their doctor, and considerably save on their medical expenses. Others can also adopt dogs to reduce heart ailments and thus prevent heart attacks. Discuss how well reasoned is this argument.

A40. This is the proverbial case of the tail wagging the dog!

It is stated that a recent survey has revealed that those who own pets, especially dogs, lead happier and healthier lives than those who do not have pets. Such people, it is asserted, suffered less from heart problems and hardly had to visit their doctor. On the basis of this, it is suggested that heart patients should immediately adopt a dog, in order to reduce the frequency of their visits to the doctor and thus save on their medical expenses. Let us see if this line of reasoning is rational.

It is more than probable that the intent of the survey was purely to measure the impact of a pet in a person's life. People do find pleasure in rearing pets, particularly dogs, as it gives them considerable emotional security. A dog is considered to be the most faithful of all animals and man's best friend. No wonder, then, that such people tend to lead fuller and happier lives than others. The mental peace and happiness thus derived tend to translate into physical well being, leading to good health. This much is understandable. However, to give a medical slant to this purely emotional exercise is surely amazing and astounding, to say the least. No medical data or proof has been advanced to even remotely justify such an outlandish conclusion. If it has been found that such people, who own dogs, suffer less from heart problems, it could be purely coincidental. Medical science has never produced any evidence to link the two, nor is there any indication to this effect in the argument. Hence the assumption is completely unfounded and irrational. It can be argued that those who own dogs tend to go out on regular morning and evening walks with their pets, and in the process better their own health, as result of this additional physical exercise. To that extent they might benefit, but to suggest that this provides a sure shield against heart problems is not believable.

It is thus quite preposterous to suggest that heart patients who do not have a dog should adopt one immediately in order to reduce their trips to the doctor, or that people in general should adopt dogs to prevent heart ailments and thereby reduce the risk of heart attacks. This would make it almost appear as if owning a dog is somewhat akin to owning a charm in order to keep ill luck at bay! Surely this cannot form the basis of any rational argument. It would seem more superstitious than scientific.

Hence, by all counts, the argument is irrational, illogical and ludicrous in nature.

Q41. A recent survey on non-profit hospitals and profit-making hospitals threw up some interesting results. While the average patient stay at the former was three days, the corresponding figure for the latter was six days. The average time for illness recovery at the non-profit hospitals was less than half the average time in the profit-making private hospitals, and the cure rate was also better at the non-profit hospitals. The ratio of employees to patients at the non-profit hospitals was much better than the ratio at the other. It was also found that there were less patient complaints at the non-profit hospitals as compared to those at the profit-making ones. This conclusively proves that the treatment and service levels at the non-profit hospitals are better than those at the profit-making private hospitals. Discuss how well reasoned is the argument.

A41. The argument has concluded on the basis of some related facts and figures that the treatment and service levels at the non-profit hospitals are better than those at the profit-making private hospitals. Let us consider each piece of information in detail to see if it is truly relevant, and if so to what extent it would influence the final conclusion.

The first fact on which the argument has relied is the average period of patient stay in hospital. It is stated that while the average period of patient stay in the non-profit hospitals is three days, the corresponding figure for profit-making hospitals is six days. It is thus presumed that patients tend to recover quicker after a hospital stay at the former as compared to the latter. However, this may be a totally misleading assumption. It is quite probable that the hospital stay at the non-profit hospitals is confined to simpler forms of illness, while the patient stay in profit-making hospitals may include hospitalisation cases of a more complicated medical nature. For example, a patient admitted to hospital for a simple fracture could be discharged in a few days time, while a patient undergoing heart or brain surgery may have to spend a couple of weeks, before he is allowed to leave hospital.

It is further stated that the time taken for illness recovery in the non-profit hospitals is less than half the time taken for recovery in profit-making hospitals. This again would depend on the type of illness. A person could recover from common flu in three to four days time, while a patient suffering from typhoid or jaundice would take many more days to recover Thus, the number of days of stay at hospital or the average time taken to recover from an illness do not in any way reflect on the superiority or inferiority of a hospital.

The second fact on which the argument has relied is the cure rate. It is pointed out that the cure rate at non-profit hospitals is much higher than that at profit-making ones. This again is debatable. Non-profit making hospitals are obviously not equipped to treat life-threatening cases, and would normally confine their treatment and hospitalisation to the relatively simpler medical cases, where the cure rate would evidently be much higher. Profit-making hospitals, on the other hand, being much better equipped on account of higher resources available, would obviously deal even with the most complicated and life-threatening cases, where the chances of recovery may be minimal. Hence the mismatch in the cure rate between the two types of hospitals.

The third fact quoted relates to the ratio of employees to the patients, which is stated to be higher in non-profit hospitals than in profit-making ones. This also could prove misleading. This could be due to a higher number of people opting to go to profit-making hospitals in anticipation of better treatment.

Finally, it is stated that there were fewer patient complaints at the non-profit hospitals than at the profit making one. This is perhaps on expected lines. After all, people who pay for their treatment are going to be much more demanding than those who receive treatment free of cost. And the majority of people who receive free treatment are more likely to feel obliged than to complain.

It is quite clear, then, from the above discussion that the apparent facts on which the line of reasoning has been structured are not exactly relevant to the final conclusion. The argument is thus weak and suffers from several infirmities.

Q42. The following appeared on the editorial page of a newspaper. Everyone is now concerned about environmental issues. Therefore, it is more than likely that Mr. Richard Jones will become the next Governor of our State, defeating the present occupant of that post by a handsome margin. This is because Mr. Jones', being the President of the Society for Healthy Environment, has vowed to adopt environment-friendly measures if voted to power. The present Governor, by not protecting the environment, has clearly done more harm to the State than good. This is obvious from the rising levels of pollution in the State due to an unprecedented rise in the number of industries, public vehicles, and construction of bridges and highways. Recently some old roadside trees were also felled to facilitate the construction of a children's hospital.

Discuss how well reasoned you find this argument.

A42. The newspaper editorial has predicted that that it was more than likely that Mr. Richard Jones, who is also the President of the Society for Healthy Environment would become the next Governor of the State, defeating the present occupant of that post by a handsome margin, as he has vowed to adopt environment friendly measures if voted to power. On the other hand, the present Governor is accused of having done more harm than good to the State, by not protecting the environment. In support of this allegation, the editorial has listed a number of concerns. Let us examine them one by one to ascertain the truth in each.

It has been contended that the level of pollution has increased on account of the unprecedented rise in the number of industries, public vehicles, and construction of bridges and highways. This of course is to be expected to some extent, because development also comes at its own price. It can never be declared that unprecedented industrial development of a state, followed by increase in number of public vehicles and construction of bridges and highways could be harmful to the interests of a State. In fact, these would be the very parameters that would determine the rapid advances made by a State. They would invariably bring greater prosperity to a state and higher levels of employment to its populace. Environment no doubt would be an issue of concern to all, but economic well-being would certainly take precedence. After all, environmental issues cannot be debated on empty stomachs. It can be asserted that the growth, which the state has witnessed under the incumbent governor, has been to a certain extent at the cost of environment, but to declare that he has caused more harm than good would be to ignore the reality of governance. Can Mr. Richard Jones who is said to be in the race of Governorship help the cause of environment in any way by retracting from the path of economic development taking place at present?

Another obvious environmental 'crime' attributed to the present Governor's regime is the felling of some old roadside trees in order to facilitate the construction of a children's hospital. This is absolutely absurd. Pray, does the felling of a few roadside trees, for a much nobler cause, result in an ecological disaster? How many trees are felled daily to be turned into pulp for newsprint or for lighting fires to heat the homes of the rich?

The argument is myopic and shortsighted because it has not been able to properly distinguish between issues of environment and development. It has failed to appreciate that both the issues are independent of each other. It is thus unconvincing and outlandish.

Q43. The following appeared in the letters to the editor column of a daily.

To increase milk production in the country, the government helped in setting up 100 new dairy farms across the country five years ago. However during the same period the price of milk in the local market has gone up from $ 2 per gallon to $3.50 per gallon. As milk is an essential item of consumption, the government should regulate the prices of milk, in order to prevent undue profiteering by the milk producers. This will ensure lower prices and sufficient supply of milk for the citizens.

Discuss how well reasoned is this argument.

A43. This argument is based on two issues. The first is the fact that the government, in order to increase milk production in the country, helped in the setting up of 100 dairy farms in the country five years ago. The second issue is that the local price of milk, during the same period has gone up from $2 to $ 3.50 per gallon. On the presumption that the milk producers are indulging in undue profiteering in spite of the increased number of dairy farms in the country, it is suggested that the government regulate the prices of milk. This, it is claimed would ensure lower prices and sufficient supply of milk for the citizens. Let us analyze both the issues to see how far the conclusion is valid and the suggestion legitimate.

In the first place, it has to be appreciated that five years have passed since the 100 new dairy farms were set up across the country. The argument has not taken into consideration the fact that the population growth in the country in these last five years would have neutralised to a great extent the additional milk supplies envisaged on account of these increased dairy farms. Further, the additional dairy farms were dispersed across the country. It is quite possible that the relevant local area where the prices have reportedly gone up from $ 2 to 3.50 actually suffers from a scarcity of supplies. It is also possible that being in some remote area, the costs of transportation may be high. It is also possible that the rise in prices is actually on account of the end suppliers, and not because of any increase on the part of the milk producers. Even if it were due to a hike by the milk producers, the argument has not considered the effects of inflation and other economic factors impacting the cost of milk production and supply. Apparently, the argument is ill-considered and flawed.

The consequent suggestion that the government regulate the prices in order to ensure low prices and adequate supplies of milk is actually self-contradictory. It has failed to comprehend that in the light of the situation discussed above, regulation of prices would not be justifiable, and if such regulation were to be enforced, the supplies would actually diminish, not increase. This is dictated by simple economic wisdom.

Hence, the argument as well as the end suggestion suffers from serious flaws of reasoning, and misplaced assumptions. Neither is the conclusion sound, nor is the suggestion legitimate.

OO

Model University Essays

Introduction

Most of the larger and more reputed Universities abroad require the prospective students who apply for admission to write essays on some topics of general interest chosen by the Universities. There are no standard issues as such, and the essay topics may differ from university to university, and also from year to year. Again, the topics given would depend to a great extent on the type of course chosen. For **management courses (MBA)**, some of the topics specifically pertain to management and career related themes.

The total number of essays could generally vary anywhere between one and five. One of the essays usually requires the prospective student to outline his career goals and explain clearly how the particular course chosen by him would help contribute to such goals. Another essay generally asks the student to provide all additional (optional) information, (other than that mentioned in the application form), which would help the selection committee to come to a decision on the application of the candidate. Sometimes the essay requires the applicant to explain why he has chosen that particular college or university to pursue his studies. An essay may also require the student to outline his short-term and long-term objectives and how he expects to achieve them.

These are subjective essays and are intended for the purpose of gaining a deeper insight into the applicant's mental framework and his intellectual caliber. Through the applicant's response, the selection committee of the college or university is able to gauge the level of his earlier learning and experience, and also judge his ability and capability to successfully pursue his presently chosen stream of study. It is also able to correlate his chosen stream of study with his future aims and objectives and thus establish his sincerity and bonafides in opting to be a student of that college or university. Through a careful reading of these essays, the members of the selection committee are also able to glean some insight into the overall character and integrity of the applicant and his commitment to the principles and ideals of the university or college and his ability to live up to them or abide by them.

From the student's perspective, these essays offer him an invaluable and excellent opportunity to impress his audience with his past achievements, both academic and otherwise, and his future goals and objectives. It gives him the chance to directly communicate with the college selection committee, and put forth before them his case for admission to the institution in lucid terms. It enables him to effectively and forcefully articulate his views, and thereby unfold before the admissions committee his passion and zeal for pursuing his chosen stream of study and his grit and determination to succeed.

It is important to remember that most of the top-notch colleges receive innumerable applications for admissions every year, invariably several times in excess of the actual intake capacity. Therefore, they are hard pressed to make the appropriate choices in the selection procedure. Under such circumstances, an impressive and striking essay can make all the difference, and help tilt the scales in favour of a particular candidate. Therefore, the vital importance of writing a good and efficient essay to effectively communicate the desired facts and details to the admissions committee cannot be belittled. In fact, it is one of the most important exercises of the entire admission process, especially for the management courses.

Model Essays

Q1. What does it mean to you to live in a global community?

A1. Time was when man lived a very lonely and relatively isolated existence. Distances were covered mostly on foot or with the help of ponies and horses. Man's needs were very few and far between. Finding food or eking out a bare living formed the very fulcrum of his existence. Marriage was between members of the same community or tribe. Man's own world was no bigger than a few square kilometers of land or sea around him, and he was quite oblivious of the great big planet that he inhabited.

The caravan of life moved on. Man evolved and progressed. Science flourished. The wheel, which once moved only the bullock cart, now began to quickly move human life itself. It was the dawn of a new era.

Civilisation today has truly come of age. The world is growing smaller by the day even as the jet engines grow more powerful. With the fading distances, gone are also man's obscurantist tendencies, isolated existences, pet prejudices, religious bigotry and myopic vision. From a mental pigmy, man has truly metamorphosed into a global giant. And the world has evolved into a global community. A community where thought is seamless thanks to the revolution in the world of communication.

Do I fit into this global mega polis? Absolutely! (Even those who don't will have to; for, there is no other space left.) There is so much to learn and so much to share - and so much to gain. Take the case of education itself. It is no longer confined to the place of one's birth. What better proof than my own application to this wonderful University for admission into its haloed portals? Take the case of religion. Bigotry has given way to understanding and tolerance. For we learn to recognise a religion not by its stone edifices but by the nobility of its teachings and followers. Gone are the barriers of caste, community, creed, untouchability, apartheid and feelings of high and low, as we all merge into the single unit called global community. Living thus, in close proximity to one another, we not only fully and uniformly share the economic, scientific and material goodies that the world at large has to offer, but are also further enriched by the developing bond of sympathy, compassion, love and sacrifice, as we begin to perceive the oneness of all the inhabitants of mother earth.

The global community truly consists of only universal beings. So, goodbye nationalities. Welcome the global citizen! Exit the man. Welcome the superman!

Q2. Do you think that the increasing commercialisation of education will rob it of its social values? If so, what should be done to prevent that?

A2. Education alone is considered to be the panacea for most of the ills afflicting society today. It is a sure remedy for the ills of rampant poverty, widespread illiteracy, unbridled superstition, religious fanaticism, cultural chauvinism, and ethnic strife, which plague most countries in the world. It is a social necessity and should be treated by all governments as a national priority. In education alone, lies hope for the teeming millions who dot the surface of this planet. Education alone holds the key to the emancipation of the vast army of the poor and downtrodden in the world. Education alone ensures liberation from the clutches of illiteracy and the grueling yoke of superstition. Education alone can rid the human mind of the cobwebs of bigotry and bias, narrow mindedness and intolerance, caste and communal animosities, and racial prejudices. It alone can rid us of the discord and strife caused by human failings born of ignorance and folly and lead us to the path of enlightened peace. It is the only beacon for a mankind, strayed from the path of sanity and immersed in an ocean of turmoil.

When so much is at stake, it is extremely disheartening to witness the crass commercialisation of education taking place today. From an ennobling occupation, education has been reduced to a moneymaking machine. The once hallowed portals of higher learning have now denigrated into cesspools of rank commercialism. Higher education today has become the prerogative of the privileged few that have the wherewithal to purchase it. For the rest, education is at best a pious dream that often remains unfulfilled. We have already said that education is a social necessity. However, if gross commercialisation takes it out of the reach of the vast multitudes, then education would have indeed been robbed of much of its social values. The very noble objective of ushering in social emancipation through education would have been defeated.

Governments have a great and onerous role to perform in this grim and sad situation. Otherwise the future of the countries over which they preside will be very gloomy indeed. They have to ensure that education, both, primary and advanced, is easily accessible to all those who desire to learn. In fact, some countries have made education up to the high school level free and compulsory for all. In a few others, even college education is free.

If it is not possible to make education entirely free for the masses, it should at least be greatly subsidised by the State, so as to ensure that even the poor can partake of it. Of what use are the resources to a State, if it cannot spend them on imparting proper education to its people? Much is spent by governments on wasteful non-plan expenditure and much is spent on unnecessary pursuits like launching space explorations and the like, yet in the noble field of education, much leaves to be desired. After all, money invested in education is money invested in the most productive assets of a nation, namely the young minds. One day these investments will bear fruit and the country will be the richer for it. What it has invested, it will recoup many times over.

Private enterprises and citizens, especially the affluent, also have a duty to perform. They cannot shirk their social responsibility towards the cause of education. It would be obligatory and in their own interests to spread education awareness as they are also part of the same society and have equal stakes in its growth and development. Their own prosperity is invariably linked to the evolution and growth of proper human resources in their country. Therefore, they should be generous in their contributions. They can greatly help by funding the growth of educational institutions and developing and maintaining them as centers of excellence. They can provide generous grants and scholarships to the needy, and loans to others who are constrained to pay later. They should also help to reserve a certain percentage of seats in their institutions for the benefit of the least privileged members of society, who can be then be educated totally free of cost. The presence of such philanthropists in its midst is indeed a great boon for any society.

To those who have turned education into a flourishing business a word of caution is due. Do not make undue profits out of the needs and necessities of people. Education is a dire need of the times, and the bulwark on which the mighty social edifice will be built. If you will weaken this foundation with your greed, then some day you run the risk of the entire structure collapsing hard on you. Therefore, please don't let the love of mammon rob education of its social values.

Q3. How does competition impact the customer and the company? Explain with the help of suitable reasons and/or examples.

A3. The prevalence of free competition in trade and industry is one of the best ways to ensure excellence in business practices, which immensely benefit not only the consumer, but also the companies themselves. The success of the capitalist model is also largely due to the forces of free competition that it encourages. In a scenario of dog-eat-dog competition, every company tries to outdo its rivals not only in offering the best products at the most competitive prices, but also by working hard to win customer loyalty by ensuring the highest level of customer service and satisfaction. In the process, the company itself undergoes visible transformation and change from within, in its quest to improve its practices with the ultimate aim of ensuring excellence in its operations.

Nothing illustrates this better than the winds of change sweeping the service industry in India, especially the telecom and banking sectors. Let us first analyze the trends in the telecom sector. Owning a telephone connection in the good old days was supposed to be a sign of luxury and affluence. One had to wait patiently for several years before one could become the proud owner of a telephone. Out-of-line connections were provided only to a privileged few like ministers, government officials, members of parliament and the like. Transfers of phone were effected at high unofficial premiums involving thousands of rupees.

Even after undergoing these heartaches, the level of service from the State monopoly provider left much to be desired. Frequent breakdowns due to poor and archaic infrastructure, wrong and excessive billing, and lack of sensitivity and proper response to customer complaints were the "perks" that inevitably came with the instrument! Then came the dawn of liberalisation, together with the accompanying competition, and today we have several prominent players in the telecom space, both in the wired and cellular domains. This has resulted in a sea change in the attitude of the erstwhile State monopoly providers. Overnight, international and long-distanced rates have been slashed to undreamt of levels due to competition from the private players. This has been made possible due to better restructuring of the organisation, better motivation of the employees, and adoption of the latest technologies to deliver a slew of products including broadband and fibre-optics at the most economical rates. Full computerisation of the organisation has minimised the risk of wrong billing, and absorption of modern technology has minimised the scourge of frequent breakdowns in service, and the menace of wrong numbers. The earlier lethargic and inefficient behaviour in the telephone offices has been replaced by a newfound responsiveness. Elegant and people- friendly customer relations centers have been created to interact with the public and attend to their queries. These welcome changes have been undoubtedly forced by the advent of free competition in the form of private players.

Let us now turn to the banking sector. The changes taking place here are as astounding as in the telecom sector. For decades, the banking public had been a silent sufferer at the hands of incompetence and inefficiency of the public sector nationalised banks. But thanks to the entry of fierce competition from the foreign multinational banks and the new-generation private sector banks in India like ICICI Bank and HDFC Bank, the entire banking scenario is now undergoing an unbelievable transformation with even the PSU Banks vying with one another to offer better options and services in order to retain customer loyalties. The results are again astounding. From being just staff-driven, these banks are being increasingly adapted to become technology-driven. Gone are the days of long and serpentine queues and dreary wait in the hot and stuffy surroundings of most banks to complete the transactions. Instead, a large number of ATM machines have been installed at various convenient locations across the country, so as to dispense with the need for the customers to frequently visit the bank branch.

The introduction of e-banking (internet-based banking) by the more aggressive and innovative players has now made it possible for customers to complete most banking transactions from the cosy confines of their own homes or offices. Banks no longer treat their customers with non-chalance, but fiercely compete with one another to offer a slew of banking products, including easily available, low interest customer-friendly loans to their customers. Customers are no longer made to sweat in hot and stuffy surroundings or sit on shabby benches, but accommodated in air-conditioned comfort amidst designer ambience.

Such startling but positive developments in these sectors have ensured that each company constantly upgrades and innovates for fear of falling by the wayside. In their constant endeavour to extend and improve the scope of their services and yet remain financially solvent, the companies have been forced to adopt sound business practices like retiring surplus and redundant labour, shedding unwanted flab wherever it exists, rationalising costs, revitalising their balance sheets by adopting prudent business norms, and ensuring the highest levels of accountability and transparency in their operations. As a result, from being long time loss-making entities, many of them have now graduated to higher rungs of profitability and growth. It is thus amply evident that competition alone can force a change for the better in business practices, if nothing else ever will.

Q4. It is said that the government's business is not to be in business. What do you think this statement means and discuss the extent to which you agree or disagree with it, with the help of suitable reasons and/or examples.

A4. Doing business with the motive of earning profits is the work of individuals and other commercial enterprises. For this, people may form themselves into partnerships or joint stock companies to raise the necessary resources and conduct their business activities. But all this remains in the private domain. However, it is not unusual to see state enterprises, generally called public sector units, operating in certain sectors on business considerations. These units are funded either entirely by the government, or with majority shareholding belonging to the government, and the rest to others. The profits or dividend payouts generated by these units are transferred to the state treasury, in proportion to the government holding in them. Public sector companies, where the government is the only or the majority shareholder, are prevalent all over the world, especially in those countries that follow the socialist model of governance. In communist countries, the government is perhaps the biggest owner of such enterprises. In capitalist countries, public sector companies are generally confined only to state utilities like railways, power distribution companies, and such others.

There is a growing belief in the world that the government should not be taking the risk of funding and running such enterprises, and that the job of business is best left to the private sector. This is what is meant by the saying, "that the government's business is not to be in business."

Do I agree or disagree with this stand? Yes and no. Primarily, it has to be admitted, that the job of doing business is best left to the private entrepreneurs. They have a stake in the profits, hence, it is fair that they take the risks and run the business. However, what stakes could a government have in running a business? Surely, profit cannot be prime motive. After all, if the same business is run by a private company, gains will still accrue to the state on account of the taxes paid by the enterprise. If such is the case, why should the government be risking public money to run a business? After all, losses are as much a part of business as are profits. What then could be the motive, and if so, is it justified? Let us analyze.

The socialist model of governance is founded on the principle of state ownership. The state is the owner and the people are the beneficiaries. The people are employed by the State, which then pays them wages for their work. Private ownership is not encouraged. This is the broad philosophy of the socialist world, though it is now gradually veering round to the concept of private ownership of business, or at least a part of it.

Some countries like India have for long followed a mix of both, the socialist and capitalist models, commonly referred to as a mixed economy. The rationale behind such an arrangement is that while the State will control and operate in those essential sectors, which are vital for the growth of the country and sustenance of the people, the other less critical sectors can be left to the private sector. This rationale is also followed, maybe in a slightly modified form, by the capitalist countries. Therefore, companies operating in public utilities field like food procurement, power generation and distribution, water supplies and maintenance, defense production and procurement, roads and highways, railways, airports, seaports, oil production, distribution and exploration and other such critical areas, are generally owned either fully or with majority shareholding by the government. This is to ensure that there is no undue profiteering in the most essential items of consumption of the common man, and also, that they are available regularly and in adequate quantities.

State control over production and distribution of oil, power and such other essentials ensure that the wheels of the economy keep moving smoothly and without any road blocks. Control over defense production, airports, and seaports are to safeguard the country's sovereignty and independence. Except in these last few critical and sensitive areas of operation, most countries have thrown open other areas to competition from the private sector. This is to make certain that there is healthy competition between the private and public sector, so that the ultimate consumer is benefited.

Viewed from this angle, government participation in certain critical and essential sectors is certainly justified. For instance, the state operates road, rail, and air services even to some of the most remote and unproductive sectors, the effort being to benefit all sections of the mobile public. Left to them, the private players would in all likelihood discontinue service on those routes that prove unprofitable to them, while retaining only the profitable ones. This would seriously impact those sections of the population living in, or wanting to travel to, the uncovered areas.

This amply justifies the government's business of being in business. After all, minding people's business is what good governance is all about.

Q5. Do you think that the primary responsibility of protecting the environment rests on the shoulders of the government and not individuals? Discuss with the help of appropriate reasons and/or examples.

A5. I believe that both the government and the individuals have an equally important role to play in protecting the environment. While the government has the larger duty of creating consciousness among the people for the need to protect the environment, and passing suitable legislation, individuals have an equally, if not more important role to play in the preservation of the environment in its pristine purity.

Why is the participation of the individuals in this joint endeavour so important? This is simply because society is always the sum total of what every individual is. Every individual is affected by his own actions and the sum total of the actions of others. So is the environment. Every single person impacts the environment, and the environment in turn impacts every single person. Hence, each and every person has a vested interest in protecting and preserving the environment. Otherwise, his own survival would be at stake. And at equal stake would be the survival of his own progeny and future generations. A sustained degradation of the environment would ultimately result in an equal deprivation for the entire human race. No one need imagine that he has got any separate existence, independent of the environment. Nature will return in equal measure what it receives from the species.

Having emphasised the individual's vital stake in the preservation of the environment, let us now try and define his role, as well as the role of the government in this worthy endeavour. The government is, after all, no more than the creation of the people themselves, and hence will act in line with their thinking. Thus, while the first inspiration must necessarily come from the people, the later impetus will automatically follow from the government. And unless the people wholeheartedly co-operate, no measures of the government, howsoever well-meaning, will succeed, particularly in this rather abstract field of environmental protection. That brings us to the question of the responsibilities of each.

The government will need to legislate against the emission of obnoxious and dangerous fumes into the atmosphere by industries in general, and through the manufacturing processes of hazardous substances in particular. It will need to ensure that vehicle emission norms are followed stringently, and actively encourage the use of alternate fuels, which result in lesser or zero emission of smoke and carbon. It will have to prevent the pollution of rivers and seas with toxic chemicals substances emitted by illegal industrial activity in the neighbourhood. It will have to avert the destruction of forests and the extinction of wildlife by the actions of a greedy few. There are, of course, many more measures that the government will have to take in diverse areas of environmental protection and preservation. All these cannot be enumerated here for want of time and convenience.

As for the individual, his role would be to call for and actively support the governmental action on the above lines, and more important by following the rules himself. For, if he will not, then all would be in vain. He can also help in a hundred different ways. First, a few don'ts. To start with, he can avoid throwing rubbish in the open and in public places. He can avoid polluting the waterways with filth and waste. He can make sure his vehicle is tested for proper emission norms. And now, a few do's. He can start planting saplings in the neighbourhood. He can use solar energy, where feasible, and thus help save the dwindling oil reserves. He can use rainwater-harvesting techniques, if available, to save the ground water levels from declining. Every single action on his part, howsoever small and innocuous looking will undoubtedly constitute a valuable link in the long chain of efforts required for the protection of the environment.

Q6. "Legislation alone will never eliminate child labour as long as there is abject poverty in society." Do you agree or disagree with this view? Discuss, giving reasons and/or examples from your own experiences, observations or readings.

A6. The sorry spectacle of a child slogging along with grown up adults in a factory or a shop is always a heart-rending sight. That children should be slaving hard and for long hours in a dingy restaurant kitchen, washing dishes or scrubbing the floor and cleaning the tables, or carrying a heavy load on their tender heads, speaks very poorly of the society that gave them a demographical belonging, yet could not provide them with the joys of childhood. Is legislation the answer to this pernicious practice, or is much more required to be done, to remove this stigma on the human conscience?

The key to the question lies in finding answers to the uppermost question of why parents send their children to the workplaces. The obvious answer that immediately comes to mind is their abject poverty. But is that the only answer? After all how much can a child earn? Surely, not the same wages that would be paid to an adult. And why can't the parents' income, however meager, provide them with subsistence, howsoever little? Perhaps we have to turn to the prevailing socio-economic factors in society for a satisfactory answer.

Most developing and underdeveloped countries suffer from high density of population and low growth levels. This leads to rampant poverty among some sections of the masses and abysmally low standards of living. This is more so in the remote areas, where opportunities for work, education and health are practically non-existent. The proliferation of large families among the poor further compounds the problem, making living conditions absolutely appalling. It is a fact that most families in these distressing circumstances subsist on hardly one meal a day. This misfortune then provides the perfect backdrop for the growth and proliferation of child labour. Children are packed off to work on farms, in factories, in shops and establishments, and in hotels and restaurants. Sometimes the work is extremely hazardous, as for instance, in firework factories. The hours of work for these unfortunate children are no lesser than for the adults and the pay extremely meager. Many a time the meager earnings brought home by these unfortunate youngsters are guzzled up in the form of cheap country liquor by the tippler father.

Another dimension, and a scarier one, to the problem is the prevalence of high levels of debt amongst these poor. Having borrowed money at absolutely usurious rates of interest from money sharks operating in these regions, entire families work as bonded labourers on farms and in factories in order to repay the loan. However, the meager wages paid to them ensure that they are never ever free even of the interest, let alone the principal. In this way they continue to slave and so do their children, sometimes stretching to generations together. Seeing the gravity of the problem, some governments have recently passed strict laws to free these bonded labourers, including children, from the clutches of the unscrupulous moneylenders. However, much more needs to be done.

It would, however, be obvious from the above facts, that the problem is much too serious to be solved by legislation alone. Even if the bonded labourers are freed by putting in place stringent laws, where do they go from there? If their economic and social situation does not improve, then they are back to square one. If the government passes blanket ban on child labour, without taking corresponding measures to mitigate the hardships of the poor, it might only lead to further misery among the affected families, including starvation and suicide.

The answer then lies in the government and civil society, together, taking proactive steps to ameliorate the lot of these unfortunate brethren, the poorest of the poor. Only if they are provided with proper employment opportunities, better educational facilities and vocational training in various disciplines can they be rescued from their present plight. Only then can we cut asunder the strong shackles that have effectively bound unfortunate innocents to the practice of child labour.

Q7. "Education alone can lead to greater emancipation among the poor masses." Discuss to what extent you agree or disagree with this. Give reasons and/or examples from your own experiences, observations or reading.

A7. Poverty is a curse for any individual or country. If it is accompanied by illiteracy, disease, and unemployment, it becomes truly debilitating. Yet, this is the fate of millions of people across the globe, whose only true possession is the misery they are born with. If the first of the three deficiencies mentioned earlier, namely, illiteracy could be satisfactorily addressed, then the other two, disease and unemployment would perhaps disappear by themselves. Let us try and understand how education alone can truly lead to greater emancipation among the poor.

True emancipation means complete freedom and liberty from all the ills afflicting a person. Most of the ills have their origin in ignorance. Just as light dispels darkness, so also education dispels ignorance. Ignorance is the all-encompassing void in a person's life, illiteracy being only one aspect of it. True education should aim to remove the entire veil of ignorance and not just teach a person to read and write.

What are the different facets of ignorance and how do they impact a person? First is illiteracy itself. This is perhaps the biggest handicap a person can suffer from. Illiteracy slams the doors of all opportunity in his face. As he is unlettered, he is doomed to a life of physical labour and menial work. He has very little chance of improving his own lot, or that of his family. Not knowing how to read and write, he has no access to any kind of knowledge. He has no idea of the opportunities that may be available to him. He has no knowledge of his rights or even his responsibilities. Thus he easily becomes a ready tool in the hands of the unscrupulous, who would like to exploit him for their own ends. He takes part in political marches, not even knowing what his party's ideology is. He loudly applauds the politicians, when they make their hollow promises, knowing fully well that his lot will continue to remain the same as before. He sells his precious vote for a pittance, when he should be voting to improve his prospects, and the prospects of others like him. What can democracy do for one, who will sell his vote to the highest bidder? The politician of course will continue to keep him tied to the yoke of illiteracy and ignorance to keep getting his precious vote, time and again.

Being ignorant, he is also superstitious. He religiously believes in whatever the local priest or the astrologer tells him. No amount of persuasion from the visiting social workers will convince him that he cannot please god by sacrificing an animal, or that his wife's illness is due to natural causes and not because of any spell of black magic cast on her by the next door neighbour. This is the second aspect of ignorance- to be steeped in superstition and mired in many obnoxious practices.

He also works hard, but earns little. Many a time, the children go without food. But that does not prevent him from guzzling the country liquor every now and then even after he learns about the deaths due to the serving of the spurious brew in the neighbouring village. He laughs it all off. He says that he believes only in destiny. And the destiny does not have any ominous bearing on him.

He does not send his children to school. He does not believe in doing so. Won't they not get spoilt in the company of others? Is it not better that they learn to work for a living? After all, it will stand them in good stead in later years.

This is the larger picture of ignorance, not just illiteracy. Just as light alone can dispel darkness, education alone can dispel this pall of gloom.

Q8. Do you believe that plastic money is fast replacing other forms of money like currency notes, coins, bank checks, demand drafts, travelers' checks, etc.? If so, will this will help to avert financial losses due to theft or fraud? Discuss with the help of specific reasons and/or examples.

A8. Though it is absolutely right to say that plastic money is fast replacing other forms of money, it would not be right to infer that plastic money can fully and completely replace the other forms of money. Nor would it be entirely right to theorise that the use of plastic money would avert financial losses due to theft or fraud. We would be able to better appreciate the significance of plastic money, if we try and compare it to other forms of money like currency notes, coins, bank checks, demand drafts, and travelers' checks and also the respective advantages or disadvantages of each.

Currency notes and coins have always been the prime form of legal tender in almost all countries. They are acceptable in all forms of transactions, big or small. They are not only a convenient form of money, but are generally equated with the concept of money itself. Money is generally considered to be a generic name for notes and coins. Currency notes and coins also constitute the most convenient mode of exchange for the common man, even if he were to be unlettered and illiterate. But it is not always expedient to carry around currency notes and coins in bulk. It is also not safe as they can be stolen. This led to the creation of other instruments of exchange like bank checks, drafts, travelers' checks and now plastic currency. While bank checks and drafts are normally used in the course of business or other dealings, travelers' checks are the preferred mode of carrying money while traveling, especially to other countries. However, the advent of plastic currency is increasingly making the usage of travelers' checks redundant and also steadily supplementing the usage of checks and drafts in business dealings, including international transactions.

The fact that plastic money is fast replacing other forms of money is also evidenced by the stupendous growth in the issue of credit and debit cards by the banks worldwide and their increasing usage by all sections of the people. The wide acceptability of plastic money is also proved by the millions of shops and establishments across the world who gladly accept and honor credit and debit cards. Plastic money is also being used to purchase products via the Internet and for other transactions involving the electronic mode. 'Smart cards' are also in vogue in many countries for usage in bus and train travel and in telephonic communication. With the fast rising preference for this mode of money, it would not be entirely surprising if plastic money were to one day greatly replace the other forms of money, or to even make them extinct altogether.

That brings us to the next question: how safe is plastic money, and to what extent can it help avert financial losses due to theft and fraud? This is a tricky question indeed. Nothing in the world is one hundred per cent safe and infallible, not even plastic money. It is convenient, no doubt, and also safe in the sense that if it is lost or stolen, the loss can be immediately reported to the card issuers, who could then invalidate its use. However, much damage could have taken place between the time it is lost and its invalidation is communicated to the member establishments. However, most banks offer indemnity to the users in the form of card insurance, which to a large extent mitigates this problem.

The other danger of deliberate misuse is more serious, though. A credit card can be easily misused by either forging the cardholder's signature or by gaining unlawful access to the card number and subsequently using the information to effect purchases or other transactions on the Internet. Cards are also sometimes misused by the owners by effecting mala-fide purchases and then deliberately defaulting on the payment. A card is supposed to offer more protection as compared to hard cash, in case of theft. However, the flip side is that if a wallet were stolen, the losses would be confined to the amount of money therein, whereas if a card is stolen, the misuse could be for substantial amounts. However, with the adoption of the latest technologies and encryption procedures, chances of frauds and misuse connected with the credit cards and the consequent financial losses can be greatly minimised, if not altogether eliminated.

The tremendous advantages associated with the use of plastic money clearly outweigh the apparent concerns.

Q9. Do you think that educational institutions should focus only on academic teaching, and not religious or social preaching? Discuss, providing reasons and/or examples from your own experience, observations or readings.

A9. I think so. People go to various educational institutions to gain academic knowledge in their chosen fields. Most of the institutions of higher learning charge substantial amount of money by way of fees for their courses. It is then only fair that the time available to the student to complete his chosen stream of study is usefully and fully deployed in academic pursuits and not frittered away in other irrelevant activities.

Further, education is a universal pursuit and all types of students go to various institutions in their quest for knowledge. Their only criterion in choosing a particular institution is its relevance to their stream of study and the availability of the courses of their choice. They are not guided by any extraneous considerations. It has also to be borne in mind that we are now living in a globalised environment, and the students, who come to the educational institutions, belong to diverse faiths and nationalities. Hence, they should not be expected or required to attend any particular sermons on religion or classes on moral or social preaching. This function is best left to the various religious institutions in the world and to the individual choice of each participant.

Again, if religious or moral preaching were to be allowed or enforced in educational institutions, it is but natural that they would incorporate in such preaching the tenets of only that religion, which is widely practiced in their respective countries. Thus, while the institutions in the Western world would propagate Christianity, those in the Muslim world would preach Islam, and those in Asia would teach Hinduism, Buddhism, Jainism or perhaps Sikhism. This will only lead to reservations, and perhaps even discord, in the minds of those participants, who belong to faiths other than that of the host country. Likewise, social and moral preaching would also inevitably encompass the beliefs and ideology of the respective country where the educational institution is located, and this may be unacceptable to participants from elsewhere.

Further, the structure of education is supposed to be built on strong secular traditions, so as to inspire friendship and camaraderie among the various participants. This laudable objective might be lost in the confusion that sometimes arises from religious debate and sermonising.

All this is not to say that ethical values should not be inculcated in the student community. But the time to achieve this is when they are still young, and the best place would be the school. It is in their early formative years that children should be taught to imbibe values that would qualify them for becoming good citizens later on in life. Here again, care should be taken to ensure that the teaching is pure and unadulterated and not tinged with any traces of religion or community.

Q10. "Free will is only a myth. Every individual is conditioned to act according to the circumstances created by his birth, schooling, and society in general." Discuss the extent to which you agree or disagree with this statement. Provide appropriate reasons and/or examples to support your viewpoint.

A10. We can say that everyone has a limited free will or acts according to a conditioned will. We lay so much emphasis on a person's individuality and free will, yet the plain simple truth is that nobody has a cent per cent free will. It is very true that every individual is conditioned to act according to the circumstances created by his birth, schooling and the society in which he lives. If it were otherwise, then every person in the world would be like every other person. All would be equally rich, healthy, happy, and act and behave like one another. It is because of the differences in their social background that individuals think and act differently, and thereby live differently. Let us see how the three main factors mentioned earlier help shape the destinies of different people.

The first and prime factor is the circumstances of one's birth. Over this the individual has absolutely no control. He is born where he is destined to be born. He can neither choose his parents, nor the place, or country of his birth. This then becomes his first limiting factor. If he is lucky to be born to rich parents, he starts off with a distinct advantage in life. On the other hand, if his parents are poor, then that becomes an inhibiting factor for him. If he is born healthy, then life would be much more pleasant, than if he were born with a congenital disease or with a physical or mental handicap. Similarly, he could be very intelligent or of poor intellect. He could be handsome or plain looking. Similarly he could be born in a rich or a poor country. If he is born in a rich country, he could enjoy certain privileges. If he were to be born in a poor country, he might have to face hardships of life. Likewise, he would enjoy all the fruits of freedom if he were born in a democracy, or suffer a life of tyranny under a dictatorship. Similarly the religion of his parents would generally determine the values and ideologies, which he would embrace in later life.

Next comes his schooling. This would now flow directly from the first factor that we have discussed above, namely, the circumstances of his birth. If his parents are rich, they could send him to the best school, where he could get an excellent education, which in turn would lay the base for his future success in life. His choices will be wider and his priorities larger. On the other hand if his parents are poor, they might send him to the local community school, which may sizably narrow down his choices in life. If he has been born in circumstance of abysmal poverty, he might even be forced to forego school and start working instead.

In this way, while the first child in our example might land a high-end job by virtue of his education, the second child might have to be content with a mediocre job. The third

146

on the other hand might be forced to do only menial jobs. But for the difference in the circumstances of their birth, all the three children could have had a similar childhood, education and future prospects in life. Who would not like to be rich and successful? But does one have the free will to decide?

The third factor pertains to the type of society one gets. This is a secondary factor and directly flows from the first and second. The first factor decides the second and the second would decide the third. Thus, if he has been born rich and attended a good school, he would constantly be in the company of children of similar backgrounds. This would then tend to condition his general outlook on life and he would begin to think, act and behave accordingly. He might be more cultured and sophisticated, and more refined in his tastes. The other two children of our example, on the other hand, will grow up in an environment that may not be so conducive, and hence will have a different outlook on life. This will then further fashion their likes and dislikes, and priorities and perspectives in life. They too would then begin to think, act and behave, in line with the tendencies developed in their earlier years. The later years of life in all the three cases will be no more than extension of the earlier years.

Thus it is that man cannot lay claim to absolutely free will. All his actions will flow from the circumstances of his birth, schooling and the society in which he has grown up. Of course, he does have the choice to break free from any particular mould in his later life. But can he do so with ease? Are any of us able to break free from the bondage of our thoughts, preconceived ideas and notions, habits, wishes and desires? Where then is the free will? If we had genuine free will, would anybody opt to remain poor, unhealthy, or unemployed? If we had a truly free will, would we not discard in a trice our weaknesses, bad habits and other failings?

This is not to say that man should always be a prisoner of his circumstances. He has to struggle to break free, and it is this struggle alone that will make him strong. He has to continuously strive to properly exercise the limited free will at his disposal to improve his lot. It is this tussle with himself and his circumstances that can ultimately make him free.

Q11. Some of the largest cities in the world suffer from acute over-population and congestion. Do you think that suitable laws should be enacted to prevent further migration of people from other smaller cities, towns, and the countryside, so as to prevent the problem from further worsening in these large metropolises? Explain with the help of suitable reasons and/or examples.

A11. It is a fact that most cities in the world are suffering from over-congestion. As a result of this, the civic amenities are getting stretched to the limit and crime is on the increase.

People have to put up with overcrowded buses and jam-packed trains. The roads are crammed with people and the traffic is unruly and dangerous. Water and power shortages are the order of the day.

Compounding the existing woes of the citizens is the steady migration of people from other smaller cities and towns to the already crammed metropolises. This not only leads to an already stressed civic administration reaching a breaking point, but also culminates in the growth of slums across the city. Unable to control the situation in any other way, some governments and even some sections of the local populace have demanded the passing of suitable laws to check the unbridled migration of people to the larger cities. How feasible is such a demand? Can it solve the existing problem or would it perhaps lead to the creation of more? Let us first analyze the causes of the migration to the larger cities, as that alone will lead us to the proper answers.

It is well known that the prime cause for the migration from the smaller towns and even the countryside is on account of the extremely poor or even non-existent employment opportunities available there. This, coupled with the lack of proper educational and health facilities and inadequate amenities, force people to migrate to cities in search of better employment opportunities and life style. Many of the villages in the countryside suffer from a total lack of even basic civic amenities like roads, electricity, drinking water, and sanitation facilities. Agriculture is the only means of livelihood for the people. It is the same story in many of the smaller towns. Transport facilities are very poor and industries are few and far between. Lack of proper schools and health centers makes the life of people here extremely hard and difficult.

The solution then lies in effectively addressing the prevailing problems of the people in the countryside and towns that force them to migrate to the larger cities. Governments should encourage and stimulate the growth of trade and industry in these remote regions by offering suitable incentives in the form of reduced taxes and duties. This will stir commercial activity and create more employment opportunities for the people, apart from bringing more goods and services to their doorstep. Similarly, schools and colleges should be set up; if necessary, with government funds and assistance. Health centers manned by qualified and well-trained staff should be established for the benefit of the local people. Substantial funds should be allocated for the development of infrastructure such as good roads, lighting, power, water, and establishment of public utilities such as road transport, railways, warehouses, and the like. Apart from aiding and facilitating the growth of industry, the development of such infrastructure would also become the means of providing unlimited employment opportunities to the local populace.

When such opportunities for growth are created in the rural areas, the motive for movement from the villages and towns is lost and migration will automatically come to an end, or at least reduce. On the other hand, if the problem is sought to be controlled through legislative action alone, without addressing the basic issues that trigger the exodus of people in the first place, there is bound to be serious discontent among the people, faced as they already are with serious problems of survival on their home turf. This then would be a very retrograde step, which will not only further enhance the hardships and suffering of the rural poor, but also breed corruption and misuse of authority, as is usually the case when such coercive legislations are enacted.

Q12. Do you feel that it is rather strange that great men, who are honored long after their death, were never recognised during their lifetime? Discuss with the help of specific reasons and examples.

A12. One of the greatest faults of history is that it almost never recognised the greatness of its tallest heroes during their lifetime. It took several years or even decades after their passing away, before succeeding generations recognised their greatness and gave them their rightful place of honor. Thus it is cynically asked by some critics if a person's greatness is understood better by those who come after him than by those who lived during his lifetime.

Why is this so? Is it due to the fact that the inherent egotism in man prevents him from recognising the achievements of another living person? Or is it that man considers it derogatory to himself to put another on a pedestal, howsoever great he might be? Or is it the ingrained sense of jealousy and envy in the human mind that is responsible for sidelining the great heroes during their lifetime. Perhaps people do not have the time or inclination to appreciate the great deeds of another, imprisoned as they are in their own petty world of human failings. It is also possible that the great men were way ahead of their times, and their message and deeds so startling and unconventional, and at variance with the mundane thinking, that the masses preferred to altogether ignore them, if not display open hostility and animosity towards them. In some cases, the great ones were actually persecuted relentlessly by the people who totally misunderstood their teachings and motives.

Leave alone mortals, even great Saints of God, who have graced this planet from time immemorial have either gone back unrecognised in their times, or worse still been ruthlessly persecuted by those very people of the times, whom they came to redeem. Let us go back in time to meet some of these greatest saviours of mankind, these revered and holy incarnations whose only mission in coming to this mortal world was to show to suffering humanity the royal road leading back to the Father.

Many centuries ago arrived the apostle of love and peace. Jesus Christ came with his message of Love, and worked painstakingly to spread the Gospel of God among the people of his land. A few recognised his greatness and became his disciples. Some others loved him for what he was and venerated him. Yet, some bigoted and blinkered people in the world thought it fit to crucify such a one on the cross. The story of many other saints is no different. Guru Nanak, a great Saint, was born in Punjab, in northern India. He too came on His Mission of Mercy, to show the Light to suffering humanity. He also faced persecution from the people of his times. One of His successors, Guru Arjun Dev, was roasted alive on a hot plate while another, Guru Teg Bahadur, was mercilessly beheaded. The great Sufi Saint Shams-I-Tabriz was burnt alive. Mansur was flayed. These great ones had no personal axe to grind. They came not for religious reasons (though religions grew later in their name), nor the worldly pursuits. They came only on a mission of mercy. Yet this is the terrible fate that their times decreed for them. Centuries later, today, they are venerated and worshipped by millions across the world, who have found in their sublime teachings, a new hope for humanity.

Perhaps this is the way of the world. It will never honor the living, but always worship the dead. It is only in their death that the great ones rise to their Glory.

Q13. "Politicians are just opportunists and politics is nothing but the art of deception." Do you share this cynicism? Discuss, citing reasons and/or examples.

A13. It is said that politics is the art of the possible. Most people also believe that politics is the art of deception. Never before have politics and politicians evoked such strong skepticism as today. If politicians and the political parties that they represent are looked down upon with such cynicism and disdain by the common people, they (the politicians) have only themselves to blame.

Time was when politics was considered to be the platform for effectively serving the people. Great world leaders and statesmen like George Washington, Mahatma Gandhi and Martin Luther King used this platform to inspire their people and rouse the spirit of freedom in them. They sanctified this podium with their own sacrifices, and with the sacrifices of millions of their countrymen who were stirred into action by their clarion call for freedom. They were history's torchbearers of freedom, who inspired through example, sacrifice and self-denial. They symbolised all that was noble in politics and political leaders. They happily underwent hardships and incarceration, so that others might see the dawn of freedom. They showed spunk in bartering their own liberty for the independence of their countrymen.

Time, however, has greatly dimmed the luminosity of the torch that they lit. Politicians today have totally forsaken the lofty ideals, which inspired these great men of history. The sheen of public service has been lost, and politics has increasingly become the path to personal power and fame. The spirit of service to the people has given way to self-enrichment and the spirit of self-denial to self-aggrandizement. No longer are politicians willing to forego their comforts for the sake of the masses they loudly profess to serve. Instead, they are swathed in thick layers of luxury and immersed in the opulence of their office. They strut about majestically on the world stage, proudly flaunting their power and position. Their sumptuous living know no bounds.

They are adept at selling dreams to the poor masses. They promise everything from food, water, power, clothing, houses, roads, buses, cars, highways, rivers, dams, to even a scintillating lifestyle for the masses. They will gladly promise the moon in exchange for the only possession of the vulnerable poor: their votes. They never care to explain where they would find the money to gift these goodies to the people. And the people never think to ask. The vote is cast and the election is won. The people are forgotten and the dream merchants return to their royal dens. The machinations of power begin on the chessboard of politics, and last till the end of their term. At the end of it all, they return to the gullible people to sell them some more dreams, and many more promises. Politics, thy name is truly deception!

They are not lacking in opportunism either. They can smell an opportunity miles away in the dwellings of the poor. They can see it in the eyes of the needy. They are quick to seize upon their problems, and mouth their pious platitudes. They do so in order to score points over their rivals. They declare that they will fight for the rights of the poor and help solve their problems, while all the time they are busy promoting their own selfish interests. They claim they will promote transparency and probity in public life, even while they keep hobnobbing secretly with the wheeler-dealers. They have mastered the art of double speak and the skill of evasiveness. Their hypocrisy goes by the name of diplomacy. They will indulge in verbal jugglery when they have to wriggle out of their promises. They will frequently swear by their own ideology and that of their party, but will not hesitate to embrace apostasy when they think it expedient to switch sides. They will keep mouthing virtues in public, while swearing all the time in private. They will loudly extol the qualities of the great men who came before them, and proudly proclaim their greatness. They will lay claim to their legacy, only till the next election they win!

Q14. "Patents tend to make medicines more expensive and thus out of the reach of the poor. Hence, they should be abolished, so as to make cheaper and newer medicines available to all." Discuss the extent to which you agree or disagree, giving reasons and/or appropriate examples.

A14. While it is undoubtedly true that patents do make medicines expensive, and sometimes even out of the reach of the poor, it would, in fact, be counter-productive to abolish them altogether, in the fond hope that this would lead to freer availability of cheaper and newer medicines to all.

It is universally recognised that the growth of medical science and the pharmaceutical sector is largely dependent on continuous research and development, which is both painstaking and expensive. Millions of dollars are spent annually by pharmaceutical companies across the world in trying to research and develop new medicines and molecules, and finding cures for a host of diseases afflicting mankind. This has become all the more imperative in recent times due to the emergence and quick proliferation of dreaded diseases like AIDS, which have mercilessly ensnared humans across the globe. Compounding the problem further is the relatively recent outbreak and spread of deadly animal-borne ailments like the mad cow disease and bird flu that have led to several fatalities in many countries of the world.

Institutes of medical research across the world are now working overtime to locate cures for these maladies and potential vaccinations for their prevention. All this calls for concerted effort and enormous resources. Though some of the richer countries allocate sizeable amounts for state-funded research, most companies have to rely on their own resources to support their activity. It is then, but natural, that the massive amount invested in such high-grade medical research activity, will translate into higher costs for the medicines produced. It has to be emphasised that but for this research effort, not many new medicines or drugs would ever see the light of day. Pharmaceutical companies who invest heavily in such crucial medical research and deliver critical products to the world at large as a result thereof, are then fully justified in demanding patents for their products, so as to be able to recoup their investments over a longer period of time through the sale of the newly discovered medicines. Therefore, to argue that patents should be abolished so as to make medicines cheaper would be like asking the farmer to sow less seeds so that he can raise a bigger crop!

Patent is the only shield available to a company to protect itself from the onslaught of cheaper and derived versions of its products in the market through the actions of those who plagiarise its processes. Thus if patents are abolished, companies would simply exit from their research-based products, as they would no longer be economically viable. The consequences of this would indeed be disastrous for the people. New medicines would become scarce and newer processes will become non-existent. This would severely affect the interests of patients worldwide and seriously cripple the delivery of effective treatment to them, leading to greater morbidity and death.

Thus, abolition of patents is no solution for making available cheaper medicines to the poor. Instead, governments should evolve a social mechanism through which the more expensive drugs could be sold to the poor and needy at state-subsidised rates through community health centers and state hospitals. The pharmaceutical companies can also come forward to voluntarily participate in this humanitarian gesture by giving a portion of their expensive patented medicines, at reduced rates, to be distributed in this manner.

Q15. "Weapons are used only to fight wars, yet ironically some countries believe that they help to ensure peace." Discuss with the help of specific reasons and/or examples.

A15. We are living in times of dual ideologies and contradictory theories. Thus it is, that some countries believe that the very weapons of war can be used to promote peace. It sounds contradictory and far-fetched, yet might be true under certain circumstances, given the strange times that we live in. Let us see if we can reconcile the inherent contradictions in this presumption, to reach an acceptable consensus.

History is witness to the fact that whenever nations have acquired substantial weaponry and military muscle, they have not hesitated to wage war against others, especially their neighbours. Weapons have always been used as a means of conquest and subjugation. They have fuelled the desire for hegemony and kindled imperialistic tendencies in the hearts of some countries. The awful wars of the previous centuries are a sure pointer to this. The relatively recent gulf wars, fought between the warring neighbours, more than a decade ago, are further evidence of the desire to dominate through the use of deadly weapons.

The cold war between the then superpowers of the world saw the infusion of deadly arsenals in the form of nuclear weapons. Though the atom bomb that was inflicted on Japan proved its deadly capacity, the newer weapons of mass destruction (WMDs), as they are called, are far more lethal in their destructive capability. It is stated that the total stockpiles of these lethal weapons of mass destruction in the world are such, that the planet can be destroyed many times over, and the human race annihilated, should they ever be put to full use. Talks and treaties for their reduction or total elimination from the world have generally proved unsuccessful. The reason given by every nuclear country for retaining these weapons is that they will help deter any forceful aggression against it and thus help it to live in peace.

This then is the contemporary theory of nuclear deterrence, so forcefully articulated in the world by the nuclear-capable states. They believe that the fear of nuclear retaliation will deter other nuclear powers, from committing aggression, or entertaining evil designs against them. They strongly feel that the danger of self-annihilation through a nuclear holocaust would be enough to throw cold water on the evil designs of any potential aggressor. In this way both could live in peace. But how does this bring peace to a country, which does not enjoy military superiority over another? Perhaps by acquiring matching military might. The logical conclusion would be that when all countries are equally strong, then wars would not serve their purpose, and would become self-defeating. Hence, to ensure peace, every country has to prepare for war! What an ironical situation! What an absurd world!

In this mad race to acquire the latest weapons to arm themselves, nations of the world are frittering away more and more resources that could help to change the plight of their poor and deprived masses. Some day in the not-too-distant future they might again be discussing how they could reduce their stockpiles or eliminate them altogether! And again the theory of deterrence would come to the fore, and induce them to accumulate more!

Q16. "The curtailment of individual freedoms for the larger good of the country is not a sign of dictatorship." Do you agree or disagree with this view? Discuss, giving reasons and/or examples.

A16. The curtailment of individual rights and freedom has always evoked serious concern among the people, and provoked loud protests from the protagonists of civil liberties in society. Diverse regimes across the world have often tampered with the rights of their civilians, many a time under the guise of national security. Whether this is a sign of dictatorship or just effective administration for the larger good of the country will be determined by the interplay of certain critical factors, such as, the type of rights curtailed, the period of curtailment, the people affected, the prevailing situation in the concerned country, the political model it follows, the role of the press and the extent of judicial freedom and activism it enjoys, through which the people can seek to redress their grievances. Again, it will depend on whether the country has actually benefited, and in what way, from such curtailment of individual rights. Let us consider each factor individually and in detail.

First, let us consider the type of rights that are sought to be curtailed and the people most likely to be affected. The most important right is the right to life and limb. If this universal right is taken away for whatever rhyme or reason, we can presume that the country is fast slipping into anarchy and dictatorship, if it is not already in it. Whenever dictators face serious challenge to their authority, they do not generally hesitate to physically eliminate their adversaries or to maim them into submission. Political prisoners are physically and mentally tortured to quell their resistance.

The second most important and fundamental right is the right to freedom. If this right is curtailed without proper and normal judicial sanction, it is again a sign of dictatorship. If individuals are incarcerated in prison for unusually long periods of time without proper charges and trial, then again it points to the prevalence of dictatorship in the country. Another important determining factor would be the type of people whose rights are

154

sought to be curtailed. If the individuals, whose rights are curtailed, are just political activists fighting for their basic rights or agitating for other political and social causes, then it is a sure sign of dictatorship. Democratic governments never curtail such activity, much less the rights of the participants in such movements. If the protests degenerate into violent behaviour, then they are treated as normal law and order problems and dealt with as such under the laws of the land.

The next issue is the prevailing political situation in the country and the political model it follows. As has been stated earlier, when fundamental rights are curtailed just to prop up a particular person or a group of persons in office or to prevent their ouster, it is deemed to be a dictatorial activity. However, a country, which is ruled democratically, may be in the throes of a severe internal or external crisis, making its very survival a question mark. This may be on account of severe social strife, civil war, insurgency or even external aggression from a hostile country. In such situations, the state normally declares a state of emergency, internal or external, depending on the factors involved and proceeds to temporarily suspend or curtail certain rights of the people in order to bring the situation under control, and prevent the country from disintegrating or drifting into chaos and anarchy. As soon as things come under control and the situation is seen to be improving, the government revokes the state of emergency and gradually restores the suspended civil rights of the people. This is normal administrative behaviour and is not to be confused with dictatorship.

Again, the political model of governance that a country follows is a very important consideration. In a democracy, it is not possible to curtail the rights of individuals, without proper judicial procedures and scrutiny. However this is not the case with countries that are ruled by dictators and despots. Some countries are even collectively ruled by local warlords and mafiosi. Obviously, civil rights would have no meaning in such places.

Another important consideration is the type of judicial system prevalent in the country. In most functional democracies the judiciary is fearless and independent. In such countries no individual rights can be curtailed in normal circumstances without legally justifiable reasons and proper judicial sanction. In countries ruled by dictators, the judicial system is largely ineffective in preventing abuse of civil rights by the state, as the judges are easily intimidated.

Some countries, which are more conservative from a religious perspective, generally impose certain restrictions on their general populace, without taking away their basic fundamental rights. These restrictions may apply to the mode of dressing and general appearance in public for men and women, behaviour in religious and public places, following of certain religious and social customs and so forth. Though restrictive of certain individual freedoms, they are not to be confused with the autocratic behaviour of

155

the dictators. Some socialist and communist regimes also impose some form of civil restrictions on their people, but this is also more due to the difference in the political ideology and the model of governance, than with dictatorship per se.

Before we conclude, we have to seriously look at some of the newly emerging trends in the world at large. The rise of the ugly face of international terrorism in recent times is a disturbing phenomenon. Never before has terrorism existed on such a wide scale or struck with such devastating and debilitating effect as in recent times. Even the most skeptical of countries have realised with some sense of shock that terrorism knows no boundaries and respects no nationalities. In their relentless fight against terrorism, some of the most affected countries have curtailed many of the civil rights of their own countrymen as also of others, who they believe are the sponsors or the perpetrators of this horrendous crime against humanity. They believe that the hardened terrorists, and other murderous elements that indulge in such atrocious behaviour against the civilized world have forfeited all claims to civil rights and liberties. They are a serious menace to society and have to be dealt with as such. Such behaviour though emanating from the democratically ruled nations is certainly not to be mixed with dictatorship. Some people strongly condemn this as state terrorism, but it has to be pondered if the menace of unbridled terrorism can be effectively countered in any other way.

In conclusion it can be surmised that the legitimate actions of the democratically elected governments, in curtailing individual rights of some sections of its people, for a limited period of time, for reasons that are widely perceived by its own people to be bona fide and in the best interests of the nation, are not a sign of dictatorship.

Q17. Do you believe that governments tend to spend most of their resources in developing only the big cities, while ignoring the villages and smaller towns, leading to lopsided growth of a country? Discuss with the help of specific reasons and/or examples.

A17. This is true of almost all countries in the world. Governments do spend a good amount of their resources on the development of big cities. However, it is not true that the villages and smaller towns are totally ignored, and no amount is spent on their development. However, the resources allocated for their development have to be in proportion to their population and growth potential. Villages and smaller towns, being sparsely populated, and widely dispersed across the country, will certainly not merit the scale of developmental resources that would have to be allocated to the bigger cities, which are home to a much larger population. Does this lead to lopsided growth of a country? Yes, maybe in the long run. However, the laws of economics will ultimately prevail and force governments to turn their attention to the development of the smaller towns and villages also. Let us see how.

In the initial stages of a country's economic or social growth, governments have to perforce plan the development strategy of the nation on a more focused basis. The limited resources have to be utilised to spur development in those places, which have a natural propensity for faster growth. The larger cities, by virtue of their being home to a much larger population, than the villages and smaller towns, would then automatically score better on that count. The prevalence of a large and educated workforce in the larger cities makes them a natural choice for the setting up of industries and other business establishments. This in turn would spur greater commercial activity leading to higher demand for civic and other amenities.

Also, some of the bigger cities, particularly those that are strategically located on the sea coast or near it, are most likely be endowed with a sea port and an airport, apart from the rail terminals. This enables them to evolve into national and international gateways, leading to an explosive growth in domestic and global trade, apart from substantial increase in passenger movement from and to the respective cities. As this will invariably lead to copious inflows of valuable foreign exchange through trade with other countries, directly benefiting the country's exchequer, the government will naturally allocate larger resources to ensure the highest level of growth in the infrastructure and other amenities in the city, to enable it to cope with the heightened economic activity and to attract the tourist potential.

Large resources will be needed not only to upgrade the facilities at the ports and rail stations, but also to construct new roads and highways, apart from widening the existing ones. Funds will also have to be spent to develop other critical infrastructure like rail and road links, connecting the ports with other important centers in the hinterland, constructing container stations and warehouses, building bridges, power stations, water and drainage networks, and subways and overbridges. With further economic growth and corresponding increase in population levels, the government would have to find extra resources to meet the ever-rising demand for more housing and other civic amenities from the citizens.

At some point, this transforms into a vicious circle. Higher spending spurs more growth, and this in turn fuels the demand for more resources to meet the city's burgeoning civic needs. Lack of employment and growth opportunities in the countryside lead to a steady migration of people from the smaller towns and villages to the prospering cities. This leads to even more congestion in an over-crowded city, already bursting at the seams and exerts unbearable pressure on the already stretched civil services like housing, water, transport and the like. This ultimately translates into serious law and order problems and social upheavals, with the local populace strongly resenting the presence and steady influx of outsiders from smaller towns and villages.

It is then that the laws of economics begin to prevail. In order to stem the existing rot and prevent further influx of people into the cities, governments will be forced to ensure economic development of the smaller towns and even villages in the countryside. The consequent growth in employment opportunities through increased business and industrial activity on account of such development will then put a partial brake on further migration to the cities. This will ultimately result in proper and even-handed growth of the entire country, with almost equal distribution of growth opportunities for all its citizens.

Q18. Do you think that the growth of science and technology has made the world a better and safer place today, than what it ever was before? Discuss with the help of reasons and/or examples.

A18. The growth of science and technology has certainly made the world a better place than it ever was before. However, it cannot be said with the same certainty that it has also made it safer than ever before. Let us understand how the rapid advancement in science and technology has impacted the world in different ways.

Let us first consider the growth in medical science. The incredible growth in this sector has brought marvelous new discoveries to the fore. The use of cutting edge technology in the medical domain has resulted in the discovery of newer cures and medicines for a host of hitherto untreatable diseases and the adoption of the very latest surgical procedures involving the least invasive techniques. As a result, treatment time for most cures has been substantially reduced and the treatment itself has become relatively cheaper, and much more effective and painless.

The adoption of the latest surgical techniques, involving the most sophisticated technology and instrumentation, has ensured safer and quicker surgery with exceedingly high rates of success and speedy recovery. The time of hospitalisation itself has been drastically reduced to the bare minimum depending on the complexities of each individual case. The great strides made in organ transplant surgery have ensured a longer and healthier life span for many patients across the world. The electrifying developments in recent times in genetic engineering, involving the mapping and manipulation of human genes, promise to propel medical science to heights undreamt of before.

Another sector, which has witnessed revolutionary developments, is the transport and communications sector. Absorption of newer technologies has made air travel safer and faster than ever before. It is the same case with surface and sea transport. Space technology has enabled scientists to explore the surface of even the distant planet Mars.

The stupendous progress made in modern communications and satellite technology has seen the advent of the Internet and Mobile culture. While the growth in wireless technology has enabled people to remain constantly connected through the use of cellular phones, the unfolding of the Internet protocol has made available boundless information resources to the people at the click of the mouse. Electronic mail has enabled the live transmission of pictures and messages in real time across the continents, obviating the need for physical mail, and the corresponding delays. This revolutionary new development has altogether changed the mode of communication between people and businesses and imparted a new impetus to trade and commerce.

Similarly, the expansion in the manufacturing technologies has seen the emergence of newer and technologically more advanced electronic products and sophisticated gadgetry for personal and home use, which have helped to elevate the general lifestyle of the people. The increased use of computerisation and even robotics in the work place has enhanced work efficiency and resulted in the delivery of almost zero-defect products and error-free services.

All these heady developments have no doubt raised the standard of living of the people and in that sense made the world a better, more comfortable, and livelier place to dwell in. But there is always a flip side to everything and so it is in the field of high technology. Just as fire is a good servant, but a bad master, so is the case with technology. Nothing illustrates this better than the advances recorded in nuclear technology. As a peacetime technology, it provides valuable alternate sources of power and energy to the fuel starved countries, but as a wartime weapon, nuclear technology can not only cause horrendous devastation of the places where it is unleashed, but also result in ghastly and horrific consequences for the affected population. It has been documented that the existing stockpiles of nuclear weapons in the world are sufficient to destroy the world many times over, and result in the total annihilation of mankind and other species. This is the chilling doomsday scenario that the world has always dreaded.

This then brings us back to the question of how well the growth of science and technology has benefited mankind. It has certainly helped to enhance the standard of living of the people, but has it actually made the world a better and safer place? Only time can tell. Suffice to say, that it is only man himself and not his machines that have to help make this world a better and safer place.

Q19. What in your opinion is the impact of television and movies on the people? Use reasons and examples to support your answer.

A19. Television and movies are an extremely powerful medium of communication and leave a profound impact on the viewers. This is especially so in the case of individuals who are more impressionable, like children and teenagers. Realising the sensitivity and gravity of the issue, most countries in the world have appointed censor boards, comprising of eminent personalities, to review every film before granting a certificate for its release.

If the movie is found to contain any objectionable scenes, such as those depicting excessive violence or vulgarity, it is cleared for release only after the offending scenes are fully or partially axed by the censor board or voluntarily modified by the producers.

Let us now discuss the actual impact that movies and television have on the people in general. Being a live medium of communication, the electronic media is able to bring real time happenings around the world right into our bedrooms in all their graphic detail. Not so long ago in the past, people around the world watched in stupefied horror as the two low-flying, hijacked jet airliners crashed into the World Trade Center in quick succession, and soon saw the twin towers disintegrate into rubble on their television screens. Not much later, the same people would have again watched in stunned disbelief, as the night sky over Iraq exploded into a thousand flames, as the American air force rained tons of high intensity bombs over the country, on the first lap of its 'Operation Shock and Awe'. Such was the impact of those live scenes of devastation, that people remember them in all their gory details even till this day.

Again, who has not been moved to tears and despair by the pathetic scenes depicting the abject poverty in parts of Africa with images of its undernourished children and famished women and men? Such live projection of the harsh reality help to create an awareness in the minds of the world populace about the extent of human suffering and the need to redress it. Again, by focusing on the burning issues of the day, impacting the lives of the affected people, the electronic media is able to effectively mould and rally public opinion, in order to compel the authorities to act. This helps to create a greater sense of awareness and activism in society in general. Programs having informative content like the quiz shows tend to improve the IQ of the knowledge-savvy.

Turning to the entertainment aspect of television and movies, scenes depicting excessive crime and violence do leave a negative impact on society, by inadvertently inciting misguided elements to take to path of lawlessness. Also, scenes portraying gross vulgarity and obscenity do rouse the baser instincts in people, and sometimes culminate in tragic cases of rape and other forms of abuse in society.

Many a time, first-time criminals have confessed that they were inspired to commit a crime after watching a particular movie. In many cases of sensational robberies, the modus operandi has been lifted right out of the movie plots. This underscores the grave influence that movies sometimes exercise over the undeveloped and juvenile minds.

Makers of films should therefore exercise the greatest caution while producing movies, so as to ensure that their films become a vehicle of social reformation and not a means of moral degradation. It should be a balanced approach of info-entertainment.

Q20. Which according to you is the most important skill that a person should possess or develop to succeed in today's world? Support your answer with reasons and examples?

A20. In an era of intense globalisation, when countries across the globe are increasingly reaching out to each other in their common pursuit of economic and political goals, and when people of diverse cultures and nationalities seek to interact with one another in furtherance of their educational, social, or business interests, the one skill which an individual will find indispensable for his success is the skill of proper and effective communication. Every individual who seeks to make a mark in his specific field of activity will perforce have to either possess this skill, or make untiring efforts to acquire and hone it. Without the aid of effective communication skills, he will discover that notwithstanding his other qualifications and qualities, he has to face insurmountable odds at every step of his life. What constitutes effective communication, and why is it so important for success? Let us see.

Communication in the most elementary sense is the transfer or exchange of thoughts and ideas through the medium of speaking, reading, writing, body language, or any other means. How effectively one is able to convey one's thoughts and ideas to his targeted audience would constitute the test of effective communication. Therefore, to enhance one's communication skills one would need to focus on all the elements of good communication, including the stated means. Speech, being the single-most important means of communication between people, it makes eminent sense to fine-tune our language skills. We should try and master the most widely used language in world communication, which at present is undoubtedly the English language. Apart from English, one should try and learn the local language of the country where one lives and works or the vernacular language of a particular area. Word power, in the form of extensive vocabulary, is as important as the grammatical correctness in the usage of any language. Only by sufficiently mastering the prime language of our communication, will we be able to conduct our business effectively and successfully. Mumbling and fumbling for words will leave a poor impression on our listeners, apart from our failure to convey the message correctly and forcefully. Similarly, one should strive to acquire proper reading and writing skills. Proper reading and writing of letters, and correct and effective drafting of various documents are essential elements in the smooth operation of any business. This is even more critical in any type of international business involving import and export of products or services. The smallest errors in the crucial letter of credit, or other important documents of exchange and negotiation in international trade can seriously jeopardise the entire transaction and result in catastrophic losses for a company.

Body language is also an important element in effective communication. It reveals several hidden thoughts, feelings, and emotions, to a keen observer, that even words sometimes would fail to convey. It helps to correctly judge the mood of the concerned person and his reaction to the overtures of another.

Proper etiquette and good manners are undoubtedly the important assets of a good communicator. He impresses by the politeness of his behaviour, not by the brazenness of his conduct. Through his well-cultivated etiquette and good manners, he is able to charm his way into the good books of others. He is also able to impress with his integrity and sincerity of purpose. A good communicator is also a very good listener, not just an effective speaker. It is through patient listening that he is able to understand the needs and requirements of another. He should also be sparse with his words, and not given to unnecessary banter. He should be unassuming, and not arrogant or overbearing in his approach.

These then, constitute some of the important elements of effective communication. Some are lucky to be born with them; others acquire them in the process of their learning or while working. Whichever way one acquires, there is no denying that good communication is the most important step to success in the dynamic world of today.

Q21. Some students prefer to attend University, while others prefer to learn through the mode of distance education. Which would you prefer and why? Explain with specific reasons and examples.

A21. Given the choice, I would certainly prefer to attend a University. There are many advantages in actually attending a University, which would not accrue to a person who prefers to learn through the mode of distance education. In some cases, the distance-learning mode would, in fact, be unsuitable and unviable, with relevance to a particular stream of study. Let us see how going to a University scores over the distance-mode.

In the very first place, going to a University provides the opportunity of face-to-face interaction with the teachers. This is extremely helpful for gaining a quick grasp of a subject, especially if it is being approached for the first time. Classroom lectures are more educative and enlightening than mere reading of written courseware due to the direct interaction between the students and the teachers. The student not only masters the contents of the prescribed lessons, but also gains a deeper insight into the subject as the teacher elucidates from his own experiences. If there are any doubts in the mind of the student, the teacher can readily offer the necessary clarifications. If he has not been able to fully comprehend any particular aspect of the lesson, he can request that it be explained to him again. Each student can also learn from the clarifications provided by the teacher in response to the doubts or questions of some other student. Students can also help each other through the exchange of ideas and information, after the class hours. Studying and working together in a group also increases the level of inspiration and quest for achievement.

Secondly, one learns in a more disciplined atmosphere. One has to attend the classes regularly and in time. This results in a more focused and systematic study. This leads to better preparation for the examinations and consequently better results. Also, one can easily access reference books and other valuable reading material from the University Library.

Apart from the academic curriculum, the student also gains by useful participation in other extra-curricular activities like sports, competitions, contests and the like. This enhanced level of participation in the activities of the university helps him to broaden his skills, and derive better emotional satisfaction. It also increases his scope of acquaintances leading to better interaction at the social and academic levels. All this helps in the sharpening of his communication skills and the overall development of his personality. He acquires more self-confidence and poise. He develops better team spirit and learns the art of working with others in a group. His perspectives on life become broader and the horizon of his thinking much wider.

Another great advantage that accrues to the university student is that of campus placement opportunities. Many reputed companies approach the good universities with offers of campus placements for their students. This is a great boon for the students, as they have the ready opportunity of direct interaction with the company managements or their recruiting agents. They are thus saved from the uncertainty and hassles of a later job hunt.

Thus, a university education is certainly packed with several privileges.

Q22. With animal diseases like mad cow disease and bird flu becoming more and more frequent in the world, and consequently endangering human life, do you think that people should now shift to vegetarianism?

A22. They should. In fact they should have done so a long time ago. The emergence of the animal diseases like mad cow disease and bird flu, and the resultant fatalities among the humans, has underscored with stunning effect, the debilitating consequences that could ensue from mindless flesh eating.

Medical research has proved time and again that the animal diet is not only harmful for the body in view of its fat content and cholesterol generating properties, but also because of its inherent toxicity. Cases of people suffering from food poisoning after the consumption of animal food are not rare. Doctors have always cautioned those suffering from heart diseases and such other serious ailments, that a fatty animal diet is extremely detrimental to their health, and have advised them to restrict, if not to altogether avoid it.

The emergence of the deadly animal diseases, which have claimed several casualties across the world in recent times, is a grim reminder of the fact that man is always at serious risk of contracting idiopathic diseases, if he persists in the practice of mindless flesh eating to pamper to his palate. In fact, his unmitigated penchant for animal flesh could cost him his very life. Another disturbing fact is the contagious nature of such diseases exploiting the spread throughout the world, from the initial place of origin, through the export of the infected meat. This spells danger not only to the people of the country where the animals have originally been infected with the deadly virus, but also to other countries across the globe.

Countries affected by this malady have responded by slaughtering the suspected animals and birds in tens of thousands. But will this perpetually solve the problem? At best, perhaps, till the next outbreak of the epidemic.

Where then lies the solution? Obviously in the shunning of animal food and turning to mother nature for a far healthier and superior diet. Vegetables abound in natural nutrients like proteins, carbohydrates, fiber, vitamins and minerals. They are lighter on the stomach, easy to digest and contain almost zero toxicity. Their utility to the body in terms of nourishment is on par with, if not higher than the animal diet. This has been medically proved. It is a great myth that a vegetarian diet is not as rich in nourishment as an animal diet. In fact it is far richer, and offers greater food variety for those who like to tickle their taste buds.

Doctors across the world have invariably endorsed a vegetarian diet for those suffering from serious heart and other ailments, and have specifically prohibited the taking of large quantities of cholesterol-saturated fatty animal food. More and more young people across the globe have realised the importance of a vegetarian diet to improve their health and control their weight. A vegetable diet has become a staple prescription in health centers everywhere and by dieticians across the world for maintenance of good health.

God gave man the discretion to choose his food and decide whether he would be carnivorous or herbivorous in his habits. This is proved by the very structure of his teeth. It is up to man now to judiciously exercise his choice after his earlier folly. If he would choose to abstain from the eating of meat, and subsist instead on a vegetable diet, he would not only be promoting his own health, but also helping to save from the butcher's knife the untold number of god's little creatures who fall prey daily to his voracious lust for the animal flesh.

Q23. You have the option of working for a big and reputed company for a lesser salary or for a small and relatively new company for a higher salary, for the same kind of job. Which one would you choose and why? Give specific reasons and/or examples to support your answer.

A23. I would prefer to work for the bigger and more reputed company even though the salary offered is lower than that of the smaller and relatively new company. I would base my choice on certain well-founded reasons.

In the first place, entry into a big and reputed company is rather difficult. Hence I would not let the constraint of a lower salary deter me from making the initial ingress into the company. I would consider the small monetary sacrifice that this decision entails as a rich investment for the future.

Secondly, the chances of a promotion and a salary hike are significantly greater in a bigger company than in a smaller one. This is because the company is likely to have substantially higher range of operations and a correspondingly higher scope of profitability than the smaller player. This significantly enhances the prospects of a periodic hike in the salaries of its employees.

Further, having a higher staff strength, the company is likely to motivate better performance among its employees through granting productivity linked bonuses or performance based incentives. This will help add to the basic pay and culminate in a higher take home pay. Again, bigger companies normally provide better perks and benefits to their employees in the form of group insurance schemes, sickness leave, hospitalisation and medical reimbursements, travel allowances, and paid vacations. Some of them even encourage their employees to upgrade their qualifications by bearing their study and training costs apart from granting study leave.

Third, the general atmosphere and work culture in the bigger and more reputed companies are far superior to that prevailing in a smaller company. The work ambience is better and the overall environment attractive and pleasant. This makes working a pleasure. The company does not cut corners in ensuring a conducive and peaceful work environment for their employees. This also results in better performance and productivity.

Fourth, working for a big and reputed company will not only boost my career prospects, but also give me better social standing and respectability. I can always talk about my company with a sense of pride and satisfaction, knowing that being a member of their staff enhances my dignity and self-esteem. This will not only give a boost to my self-confidence but also provide me with a sense of inner well-being.

Fifth, a bigger and more reputed company, by virtue of its greater business stability and financial muscle and strength, can easily sail through any adverse economic period or any other internal or external crisis without loosing its mooring. This endows the job with greater stability and permanence, and thus ensures greater peace and contentment for its employees.

Surely, the advantages of working for a bigger and more reputed company far outweigh those temporary temptations of an initially higher salary, which also may not be sustainable over a longer period of time due to the inherent weaknesses and fragilities associated with a small and relatively new company.

Q24. Given the choice, would you like to be a self-employed professional, own a business, or work for someone else? Explain with the help of specific reasons and/or examples.

A24. If destiny ever favoured me with a choice, I would like to be a self-employed professional. Actually a professional is very uniquely placed. He could enjoy the best of all the three worlds. By dint of his superior qualifications and specialised knowledge, he would be able to easily find an exclusive job, which would be relevant to his specific domain. In course of time, after acquiring the necessary resources and experience, he could graduate to setting up his own practice, or business as the case may be.

Let's take the case of a doctor or an engineer. A doctor generally has to work in a public hospital for a specified number of years after graduation, before he can set up his own practice. He can continue working in the same place thereafter, or shift to a better paying private hospital. If he so desires, he can also set up his independent practice or consultancy. Similarly, an engineer after graduation would like to initially work in a factory to acquire the needed work experience and proficiency. Thereafter, he could set up his own engineering firm, provided he has the required resources and business expertise. The same would apply to a lawyer, a chartered accountant, and every other professional. Hence, a professional enjoys greater flexibility in his mode of operation.

A professional is also better placed than an ordinary employee in work hierarchy. By virtue of his superior skills, he generally enjoys higher earnings and has a greater say in the conduct of the operations, which are relevant to his specific domain. Hence, within a hospital, the key figure is always the doctor himself. All others, howsoever placed, play only a supporting role. This would be true of the hospital administrators, the nurses, the supervisors, and all other employees. Similarly, the lawyer is always the central figure in any law office, though the others may perform subsidiary or sundry functions. This lends an aura of exclusivity to a professional.

A professional can also decide his own work timings as best suit his convenience, if he has his own practice. Thus, a doctor who is working in a public or private hospital during the morning hours can be free to see patients in his private clinic during the evening hours. If he is a full time private practitioner, he can split his hours of consultation both during the morning and evening. If he is a visiting consultant, he could choose the timing and days of consultation in different hospitals or clinics. This flexibility of timing gives a lot of room for efficient work maneuverability to a professional.

A professional by virtue of his specialised qualifications can also impart his knowledge and skills to others by teaching at the relevant institutes. Thus, many senior medical men are not only practicing doctors but also specialist professors in several medical institutions. This results in tremendous personal and professional satisfaction to the concerned professionals.

Finally, the greatest assets of a professional are the specialised knowledge and skills that he has acquired in the course of his education and practice. These are his lifelong treasure, which no one can ever steal from him or deprive him of. He can set up his practice whenever he wishes and wherever he wishes. He is not subject to the vagaries of a job market or the fluctuating fortunes of a business cycle. His career model is more stable and dependable. His children can readily benefit from his experience and continue his line of practice if they so desire and qualify. Thus, the whole family benefits, as does society in general, from the presence of a professional.

Q25. How does education ensure success in life? Discuss with the help of specific reasons and/or examples.

A25. Education is indeed the single most important contributor towards a successful life. It constitutes the very foundation on which the edifice of our career can be built. It opens the window to limitless opportunities in the world. It not only uncovers the latent skills in an individual, but also helps light the lamp of knowledge within him. It enhances his personality and equips him with the confidence to face the challenges of life bravely and boldly.

Let us delve deep into this ocean called education and try and discover the treasures that lie hidden within.

Education can easily be linked to the concept of wealth creation in modern society. In earlier times, wealth was normally associated with the possession of land, building, gold, silver, automobiles, and the like. These were bequeathed as heirlooms from father to son, and from one generation to another to retain prosperity in the family. The land could either be used to grow crops or build houses. The landed classes who constituted the wealthy segment of society usually employed the poor to work on their farms at very meager wages or lent out their lands at usurious rates to the non-landed farmers for cultivation. This resulted in great exploitation of the poor and led to class conflicts, as one section of society continued to prosper at the cost of another. While the landed rich grew richer, the landless poor grew poorer.

Fortunately, education has changed all that and restored more equilibrium in society by ensuring equal opportunities for all. Today, even the least privileged can seek to do better in life purely on the strength of their education. By being able to access good and well paying jobs on the strength of their educational qualifications, they can expect to gradually move up the ladder of success in life and create wealth for themselves and their families which was denied to them earlier.

Good education is also a pre-requisite for successful management of one's resources. After all, wealth creation must inevitably lead to proper wealth management; otherwise, the very purpose of wealth creation is defeated. Only a skillful management of one's wealth can help it to grow with safety and stability, and for this one has to be knowledgeable enough to be able to wade through a plethora of business and investment opportunities that exist today and make the right choices. Proper education alone would help to achieve this objective with ease.

Education thus helps to provide a level playing field for everyone, and this in turn removes the root cause for class formations and other aberrations leading to tension in civil society. This then is the second major benefit flowing directly from education. It helps to foster peace and tranquility in civil society and thereby helps the individual to make further economic and social progress.

Further, modern civilisation has thrown up limitless opportunities for those who work hard enough to uncover them. Proper education alone enables and equips an individual to fully identify and exploit the potential of such opportunities. These great new opportunities stretch all the way from the marvels of modern engineering and the wonders of genetic restructuring, to the unraveling of the mysteries of the red planet in space. The wired world of yesterday has made way for the new seamless world of cyberspace, where data can be stored and transmitted without limit and across continents in a flash at the click of a mouse. This has resulted in a seamless migration of hi-tech jobs across the international frontiers through the portals of cyber-space.

The ability to capitalise on these unlimited opportunities of out-sourcing is also limited only to those who have acquired international skills through proper education. There is no dearth of such people though, who through the sheer use of their educational skills and enterprise have managed to fully exploit the wonders of modern science, and in the process, created value-added growth for themselves and the world. Thus, Microsoft was born out of the creative genius of its founder, Bill Gates. Similarly, the concept of free e-mail was introduced by the innovative urge of Sabeer Bhatia. The same story has been repeated time and again in the domains of modern medicine, nuclear technology, space research and numerous other fields. The common thread running through all these priceless endeavours is nothing but professional excellence acquired through rigorous education.

The processes of production and manufacture and even services in the present day world have been reduced to a high grade of specialisation. It is imperative then that one needs to be sufficiently skilled to be part of the modern workforce that churns the new economy. This again is possible only through proper education, which not only helps to uncover the latent skills in an individual, but also aids in sufficiently developing them.

Let us now look at another important dimension of education. Education, apart from furthering the career goals of an individual, also serves to greatly enhance his overall personality and outlook. It equips him with the confidence required to face the varied challenges of modern civilisation bravely and boldly. The overall level of learning acquired through his education gives him the wisdom to effectively tackle the pulls and pressures of daily life, and remain calm and unruffled in the face of stressful and adverse situations. His superior skills and analytical abilities enable him to comprehend and solve the complex problems of life with understanding and ingenuity. The insight acquired by him into human behaviour and psychology in the course of his long years of education help him to interact better and more meaningfully with a cross-section of people. His superior communication skills help him to project his views to others more effectively and usefully. With a heightened sense of awareness of his rights and duties, he is not vulnerable to the machinations of his rivals or to exploitation by others. His outlook is broad and free of petty prejudices and biases. His view of things and events is rational and he shuns superstition and other irrational practices. This attitudinal change in him definitely ensures a greater degree of success in his life.

Let us now consider the social implications of good education for a successful life. It is widely recognised and accepted that good education does not consist of just learning and mastery of the academic curriculum in school or college, but also the assimilation of a complete system of values and ethics. This alone adds soul to one's education and makes him a complete human being. It enhances his power of discrimination and helps him to rationalise between desirable and undesirable behaviour. It helps to broaden his vision and elevate his thought. When he has thus transformed himself, he is also assured of success in his personal, professional, and social life. After all, success cannot be measured in monetary terms alone. An educated person is also an asset to society in general. His special skills can be usefully deployed for the benefit of society in general and the less privileged in particular. This brings honour and recognition to an individual, which is also a measure of his success in life.

Thus it can be surmised that education does ensure success in life in all its aspects.

∞

Improve Your WORD POWER
A concise way to increase your word power

—*Clifford Sawhney*

English is a unique language which has innumerable great poets and authors from the past as well as the present, who have contributed profusely to its rich heritage. Nonetheless, we cannot ignore the complexities of the English language which sometimes perplex a reader or even a scholar of this language.

Improve Your Word Power by Clifford Sawhney simplifies all these complexities of the language by providing answers to the many nagging grammatical queries, syntax, style, choice of words, spellings, etc. This book serves as a complete guide and elaborately explains the different usages of nouns, adjectives, adverbs, phrases, proverbs and so on. Hence, it will undoubtedly serve as a bible for both the lovers and wizards of English language.

Pages: 232 • Price: Rs. 80/-
Postage: Rs. 15/-

Best-sellers Books

Life is always the greatest teacher. But reading about the experiences and words of others is also a great form of learning. The wise and witty quotes in this book can teach one more in a few hours' reading than a lifetime of bumbling around. Many of the quotes are uncommon and will not have been read before by most readers.

The Book of Uncommon Quips & Quotations also includes meaningful proverbs, poems and limericks. The focus of this book, though, is more on animals, nature and man. Many quotes stress the importance of compassion towards all our fellow creatures that inhabit the earth. The quotations include those of celebrity authors, poets, presidents, musicians, film stars, humorists and others.

Pages: 128
Price: 80/-

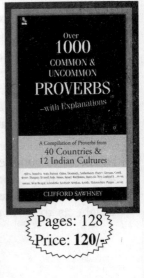

Over 1,000 fully annotated proverbs
The only book to list proverbs by country and culture
Plus scores of English equivalent sayings quoted throughout.

While there are numerous Indian and foreign books on proverbs, what sets this book apart is that this is the only one to list proverbs by country and culture with entries from A to Z. Besides, many of the annotations are comprehensive with extra information on certain cultures and customs, which will enhance readers' general knowledge. And readers seeking proverbs on specific topics can simply flip to the Index and find what they are looking for.

Furthermore, the emphasis of this book is on uncommon proverbs, which ensures readers more value for money. There is a special section on Indian sayings, under the heading, *Oriental Proverbs*. The book contains almost 25 per cent Indian proverbs. The universal insights and moral teachings in these proverbs will undoubtedly help readers broaden their mental and spiritual horizons.

Pages: 128
Price: 120/-

Postage: Rs. 15/- each book

Group Discussion
For Admissions & Jobs

—Anand Ganguly

A good score in Group Discussion
can ensure the critical edge you are looking for over other contenders

Does the aggressive speaker lead the way in a group discussion? Or the one who speaks more? Or the one who argues in favour of the subject?

Perhaps none! There are many myths prevalent about group discussions, and only the one who has seen it all from the other side of the table can guide you the right way!

Anand Ganguly, who has held senior positions in MNCs, is surely in the right position to offer you correct perspective and advice on the subject.

In this well-researched book, he has put in the essence of his decades of corporate experience into a comprehensive and complete volume on the subject. Beginning from common myths about group discussions, the Do's and Don'ts of the test, he goes on to discuss at length about the prerequisites for preparation such as knowledge of the subject, importance of listening, presentation, initiation, body language, communication skills and co-operation.

In addition, the book offers you a comprehensive background on major relevant topics from generic drugs to pension reforms, from criminalisation of politics to sex education. Above all you have 24 mock group discussions with detailed analysis and evaluation of speaker's approach and capability — offering an insight as to how to avoid the pitfalls and come out a winner.

Demy Size • Pages: 200
Price: Rs.108/- • Postage: Rs. 15/-

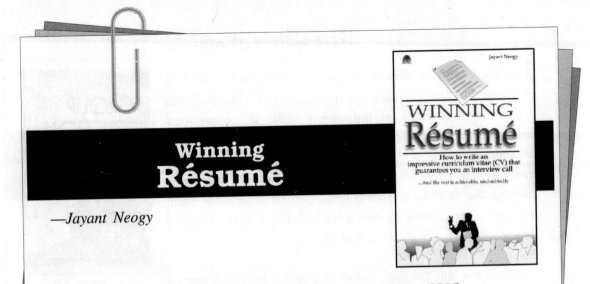

Winning
Résumé

—*Jayant Neogy*

How to write an impressive Curriculum Vitae (CV)
that guarantees you an interview call
...And the rest is achievable, undoubtedly.

Your résumé is your first introduction to the employer who has never seen you before. You need to give it the best shot to make the first winning move. The book 'Winning Résumé' fulfils this long-felt need for a contemporary guide on résumé writing that is in line with the expectations of global employers in this information technology driven age. The book breaks away from the traditional world of sequential cataloguing of degrees and job histories. Instead, it provides candidates seeking new jobs or job changes with contemporary techniques to fulfil a difficult task, to produce polished, subtle and refined advertisement- copy about their own selves.

This book is the result of an extensive research, practical experience and deep insight. There are practical guidelines for crafting a winning résumé that will stand out amongst a thousand others. Key points are highlighted throughout the book by using bold text on the left side of paragraphs; useful "tips" are identified by figures of a wise owl. To point out errors and grave mistakes in résumés "traps" are identified by figures of skull and crossbones. After going through the book the readers will get a thorough understanding of the changes in philosophy and techniques that have revolutionized presentation of curriculum vitae. It is a sure-shot for success in one's pursuit of an illustrious career.

Demy Size • Pages: 136
Price: Rs. 96/- • Postage: Rs. 15/-

Best-sellers Books

The book aims to display uncommon expressions that look common but are uncommon in usage and meaning. The uncommon expressions are interwoven within he conversations fitted into suitable situations. Dialogues containing common and uncommon expressions, phrases and idioms are developed in a most fascinating style displaying a rich vocabulary and appropriate language that provides a modern touch. In this respect, the reader will have a face chance to experience varied and trying situations during different sets of conversations.

The book not only provides new vistas of vision as regards learning how to converse with the people, but also extends before the reader new sets of situations knitted in dialogues enabling one to enrich his/her linguistic capabilities.

WORDS & PHRASES
that carry
UNCOMMON MEANINGS

Pages: 136
Price: 50/-

GMAT, GRE & TOEFL

✓ This booklet is intended to teach how to reduce the errors that occur in the Sentence Correction Test for Admission to Foreign Universities.

✓ It also teaches us how to locate the various types of errors in sentences.

✓ The basic rules of Grammar have been explained briefly and systematically.

✓ The examples and exercises given in this booklet will make you familiar with the different types of questions and provide you with sufficient practice to use the different techniques for answering each type of question.

✓ There is also a practice test to evaluate your progress and make you perfect.

Sentence Correction
for admission
to
Foreign Universities

GMAT, GRE & TOEFL

A. P. SHARMA

Pages: 168
Price: *80/-*

Postage: Rs. 15/- each book

Dictionary of Modern Phrases with Meanings & Usage

—Joel Lyall

Arranged in Alphabetical Order

The beauty of any language lies in the appropriate usage of a word or phrase. English, too, has its norms and nuances, and one should know the exact meaning and implication of each word. Many words and phrases have intriguing meanings that may not be apparent at first glance.

This is a unique book of its kind, making its appearance in India for the first time. It is a diligent compilation of modern phrases currently in use the world over. The illustrative examples make understanding easy.

This book of modern phrases will help you hone up your grasp and command over the language and pack a punch in your speech and writing.

A must for all those who wish to improve their English and communication skill.

Pages: 208
Price: Rs. 96/-
Postage: Rs. 15/-

2000 English Phrases & Sentences for all situations

—Colonel Rajeev Mongia

Improve your written & spoken English

The 2,000 phrases and sentences in this book highlight the rich tapestry of expressions in the English language. Many words and phrases have intriguing meanings that may not be apparent or register at first glance. Some words have contrasting meanings in different situations. Yet others are just the opposite of what the word or sentence seems to suggest!

The book is categorised into 12 segments that classify sentences into various types. This facilitates the reader's search for the correct sentence in specific scenarios and the book can be used as a reference guide to find the right sentence, much like a dictionary used for words.

2000 English Phrases and Sentences will enhance the written and spoken English of the readers. Besides, the book will be of immense help to almost everyone from all walks of life, including schoolchildren, college students, parents, teachers and various other professionals.

Pages: 128
Price: Rs. 80/-
Postage: Rs. 15/-